Student Book

Blueprint

1

A1 Beginner

Eric Williams · August Niederhaus

Contents

* Also, see the glossary in the back of the Workbook.

iii

Contents

Grammar and Structures	Listening / Reading	Writing / Speaking
Lesson 1 *what time* questions and their answers	**R&L**: Reading about the details of people's routines	**S**: Telling time
Lesson 2 Simple present: *go* and *do*; *before* and *after* phrases	**R**: Reading clocks to tell time	**S**: Talking about when things happen
Lesson 3 *how often* and adverbs of frequency	**R**: Labeled pictures	**W**: Filling out a class schedule
Lesson 4 More *where* questions and their answers	**R&L**: Descriptions of buildings	**W&S**: Describing habits
Lesson 5 More *how* questions and their answers	**R&L**: Reading and listening to directions	**S**: Describing buildings
		W: Writing directions and drawing a map
		W: Describing other people's routines
Lesson 1 Adjectives and linking verbs	**R&L**: Descriptions of buildings on campus and places inside them	**W&S**: Describing rooms, offices, and other places in a building
Lesson 2 Adjectives before nouns	**R&L**: A phone conversation	**S**: Pronouncing phone numbers and other numbers
Lesson 3 Adverbs of frequency with *be*	**L**: Taking notes on things you hear	**W&S**: Having a short conversation by phone
Lesson 4 More *how* questions: *how* + adjective/adverb	**R&L**: Conversations asking for information	**W&S**: Using notes to help you describe a place
Lesson 5 Intensifiers	**R**: A university brochure	**S**: Asking questions to get information
		W&S: Describing weather and places that are outside
Lesson 1 Present continuous tense	**R&L**: A conversation about where someone is going	**S**: Discussing what people and animals are doing
Lesson 2 *want and would like*	**R&L**: A request for help from a librarian	**S**: Discussing what you want or would like
Lesson 3 Questions with *what* and *what kind (of)*	**R&L**: Conversations about what to eat or drink	**S**: Talking about food, cooking, and eating
Lesson 4 Questions with *what* and *which*	**L**: People ordering food in a restaurant	**W**: Taking notes and using them to write a paragraph
Lesson 5 Questions with *how many* and *how much*; uncountable nouns	**R**: Reading about books in a bookstore	**S**: Listing things you buy or want
		W&S: Things you want to do
		S: Discussing what is required for certain activities
		S: Role-playing a transaction in a bookstore
Lesson 1 Present continuous in information questions, including subject questions	**R&L**: A conversation between a taxi driver and a passenger	**S**: Giving an address
Lesson 2 Negative imperatives; conjunction *or*	**R**: Reading signs	**S**: Talking about people who are going places
Lesson 3 Conjunctions *and* and *but*	**R&L**: Reading paragraphs and listening to monologues	**W**: Writing classroom rules
Lesson 4 Simple present: *like* in statements and questions	**L**: Descriptions of houses	**S**: Describing houses
Lesson 5 Simple present: *can*	**R**: A description of how to make an omelet	**W&S**: Listing and discussing hobbies
	R: An advertisement for a house	**W&S**: Taking notes and talking about things you and your classmates can do
		W: Writing a how-to paragraph
		W: Writing an advertisement

A NEW CLASS

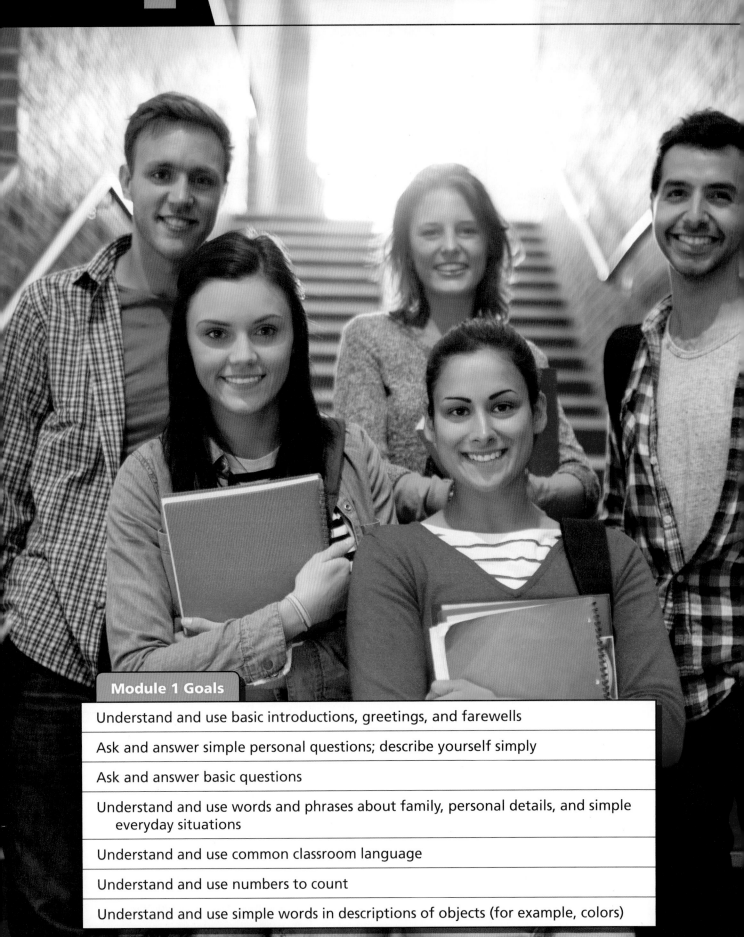

Module 1 Goals

Understand and use basic introductions, greetings, and farewells

Ask and answer simple personal questions; describe yourself simply

Ask and answer basic questions

Understand and use words and phrases about family, personal details, and simple everyday situations

Understand and use common classroom language

Understand and use numbers to count

Understand and use simple words in descriptions of objects (for example, colors)

Preview

Look at pages 8 to 33. What pages are these things on?

names of colors   _____

a green clock   _____

telephones   _____

a truck   _____

Discuss

Talk about the questions with a partner.

1. Do you think the people are workers or students?
   I think the … are …

2. In English, what is the name of your country?
   In …, the name of my country is …

3. What's the name of your language?
   The … of my language is …

4. What are some greetings in your language?
   In my language, … and … are greetings.

5. Do you greet your teachers in your language or in English?
   I greet my teachers in …

   _____

Unit 1

Unit 2

Scan the QR code to watch a preview video.

Lesson 1	What's your name?

A Model Conversation

Read the conversation. Then listen. Track 02

Woman: Hello. Are you the tutor?

Man: Yes, I am. Are you here for tutoring?

Woman: Yeah. Is it just me?

Man: No, I have a list of seven names here. What's yours?

Woman: It's Maya.

Man: Maya. Yep, right here. Your last name is Mandelli, right?

Maya: Yeah, that's me.

Man: Great. My name's Martín, by the way. Martín Abreu.

B Vocabulary: People

Study the words. Then listen to the conversation again and fill in the blanks. Track 02

girl

boy

woman

man

← People

People at school →

student

teacher

classmates

tutor

1. Maya is the ⓐ _____. She is a ⓑ _____. Her ⓒ _____ name is Mandelli.

2. The ⓐ _____ is Martín. His last ⓑ _____ is Abreu. He is a ⓒ _____.

3. They ⓐ _____ not ⓑ _____.

C In Your World

Look at the name tags. Write your first name and last name on a tag. Then choose a partner. Ask his or her name and design a name tag for him or her.

What is your name?

HELLO!
My name is

What is your partner's name?

HELLO!
My name is

D Grammar

Simple present: *be*

Brief note

Use *he* for a man, *she* for a woman, and *it* for a thing.

be questions	answers to *be* questions	*be* statements
Am I a student?	✓ Yes, you **are** (a student).	You**'re** a student.
Are you a teacher?	✗ No, **I'm not** (a teacher).	**I'm not** a teacher.
Is he a man?	✓ Yeah (, he**'s** a man).	He**'s** a man.
Are we classmates?	✗ Nope (, you**'re not** classmates).	You**'re not** classmates.
Are you girls?	✓ Yep (, we**'re** girls).	We**'re** girls.
Are they friends?	✗ No, they **aren't** (friends).	They **aren't** friends.

Brief note

Yep, yeah, and *nope* are informal. Use them with your friends.

E Grammar Practice

Write *be* questions. Then (circle *yes* or *no* and) fill in the blanks.

1. Q: _____ you John?   A: (Yes / No), _____ Daniel.
2. Q: _____ you teachers?   A: (Yes / No), _____ are teachers.
3. Q: _____ he your boss?   A: Yes, _____ is my _____.
4. Q: Are _____ our teacher?   A: Yes, I'm _____ teacher.
5. Q: Is _____ your dog?   A: No. _____ a cat.

F Use the Language

Introductions

1. Think of your first meeting with an important person—a friend, your boyfriend or girlfriend, your boss, etc. Write the first conversation between you and that person.

A: _____

_____

B: _____

_____

A: _____

_____

B: _____

_____

2. Choose a partner. Role-play your conversation.

A   Model Conversation

Read the conversation. Then listen. ● Track 03

Woman:	Hi. Is this the chemistry class?
Man:	Yep, it sure is.
Woman:	Great. I'm Bren. So, you're in this class too? Then we're classmates. What's your name?
Man:	Oh. No, we're not classmates, actually. I'm not a student. I'm the teacher.
Bren:	Aha. The teacher. Sorry. That's embarrassing.
Man:	No, don't be embarrassed. It's not a problem. Anyway, I'm Mr. Pearl.
Bren:	Mr. Pearl. Well, it's good to meet you, Mr. Pearl.
Mr. Pearl:	Good to meet you too, Bren. So, are you a new student?
Bren:	Yeah, it's my first day in this school.
Mr. Pearl:	Well, welcome to chemistry class.

B   Vocabulary

Study the expressions. Then fill in the blanks, and then listen. ● Track 04

Greetings		Other common expressions
Hello. Hi. Hey. **Brief note** *Hey* is informal.		Please ⌐ People ⊢ call me (name). (But) You can ⌐
Q: How's it going? / How are you (doing)? A: (I'm…) (Very) Well/Good. Not bad. Okay. All right. (Thanks.)		Q: How/What about ⌐ ⊢ you? A: Me too. / Not me. Q: And ⌐
Good morning/afternoon. It's good to see you.		I'm sorry. What? / Could you repeat that?
Introductions		
Nice/Good to meet you. Welcome. I'm… / My name is… I'm new here. / I'm a new student here.		

1. Man: **ⓐ** _____ morning, Cynthia.
    Cynthia: Hey, Frank. How **ⓑ** _____ you?
    Frank: Not **ⓒ** _____, thanks. And you?
    Cynthia: I'm all right.

2. Man: Hi. I'm Robert Dixon, but please **ⓐ** _____ me Bob. I'm a new teacher **ⓑ** _____.
    Woman: It's nice to **ⓒ** _____ you, Bob.

C   About You

Circle the correct answer. Then fill in the blank.

1. I (am / am not) a new student here.

2. People call me _____.

D Grammar

Short forms (contractions)

subject pronouns	*be* verbs	short forms
I	am	I'm
you	are	you're
he / she / it	is	he's / she's / it's
we	are	we're
you (guys/all)	are	you're
they	are	they're

> **Brief note**
> Use short forms often. Use long forms (subject pronoun + *be*) to highlight.

> **Brief note**
> *You* can mean one person or many people. Americans often say *you guys* or *you all* for more than one person.

E Grammar Practice

Look at the model conversation and fill in the blanks with the long forms.

1. Hello. _____ _____ Bren.

2. _____ _____ a new student.

3. _____ _____ not classmates.

4. _____ _____ the teacher.

F Pronunciation

Short forms and intonation ⊙ Track 05

1. Listen to the conversations. Look at the <u>underlined</u> words. Does the speaker use the long form or the short form? Why?

My <u>name's</u> John.

I'm sorry. What?

My <u>name is</u> John!

<u>You are</u> not. You're a student, too.

Are you a new student? I'm the teacher.

2. Listen again and repeat.

G Listen to Speak

Listen to two conversations. Which conversation matches the picture? Why do you think so? ⊙ Track 06

Tell your partner. Does your partner agree? Why or why not? Write.

_____

_____

_____

_____

_____

_____

11

A   Model Conversation

Read the conversation. Then listen. 🔘 Track 07

Woman:	Hello, Mr. Garza.
Mr. Garza:	Oh. Hi, Miss Wells. Please call me Jimmy.
Miss Wells:	Okay, then you can call me Angela.
Jimmy:	All right. And how are you today, Angela?
Angela:	I'm good, Jimmy. What about you?
Jimmy:	Yeah, I'm okay too. Is the teacher here?
Angela:	Mrs. Watson? I don't know. I don't see her.

B   Vocabulary

Study the words and phrases. Listen and repeat. Then try to add more jobs. 🔘 Track 08

Marital status

husband   wife

married

single

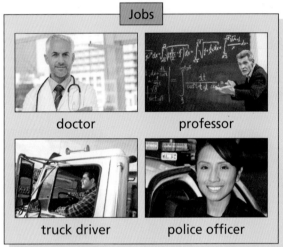

Jobs

doctor   professor

truck driver   police officer

Other jobs

C   Vocabulary: Titles

man: Mister (Mr.)	woman: Ms.
married woman: Mrs.	unmarried woman: Miss

medical doctor or PhD: Doctor (Dr.)
university professor: Professor (Prof.)

Listen and practice. 🔘 Track 09

1. Mr. & Mrs. Smith   4. Dr. Jones
2. Prof. Alvarez   5. Miss Perkins
3. Ms. Green

D   About You

Fill out the first part of a visa application form.

What country are you going to?

_____

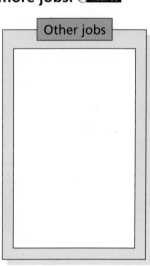

VISA APPLICATION

Visa application time: 9:00–11:00 a.m. M-F
Visa pick-up time: 11:00 a.m.–12:00 p.m. M-F

Part 1: Personal Information

Title Mr. ___ Mrs. ___ Miss ___ Ms. ___
Marital Status Single ___ Married ___ Divorced ___ Widow(er) ___ Other ___

Name Given Name (First Name)	Surname (Family Name)

Grammar

Short forms (contractions) in negative statements

short forms in negative statements	
I'm **not**	we're **not** / we **aren't**
you're **not** / you **aren't**	you're **not** / you **aren't**
he's **not** / he **isn't**	
she's **not** / she **isn't**	they're **not** / they **aren't**
it's **not** / it **isn't**	

F **Grammar Practice**

Fill in the blanks with a short form or a title.

1. I'm Jimmy. I'm a student. _____ _____ a truck driver.

2. Angela Wells is single. S_____ _____ married. _____ Wells is a student.

3. The teacher is a woman. S_____ _____ a man. _____ married. Her name is _____ Watson.

G **Use the Language**

Introducing other people

1. Give the people names, jobs, and titles. Are they married?

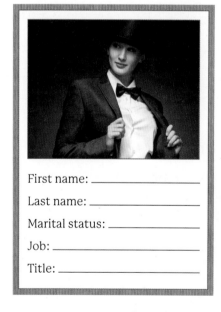

First name: _____
Last name: _____
Marital status: _____
Job: _____
Title: _____

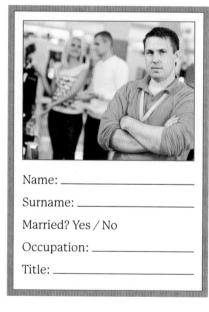

Name: _____
Surname: _____
Married? Yes / No
Occupation: _____
Title: _____

Given name: _____
Family name: _____
Married / Unmarried
Career: _____
Title: _____

2. Choose a partner. Take turns introducing the people above to your partner. Use affirmative and negative statements.

3. Write an introduction about one of your partner's people.

_____

_____

_____

_____

_____

A Model Conversation

Read the conversation. Then listen. 🔘 **Track 10**

Advisor: Hi. Are you here for an advising appointment?

Woman: Yes, I am.

Advisor: Great. And your name is Biyu?

Woman: Yes, that's right.

Advisor: That's a pretty name. What's your last name, Biyu?

Biyu: It's Yang.

Advisor: Oh. Are you from Korea? I have a lot of students from there.

Biyu: I'm actually from Peru. But my parents are Chinese.

Advisor: Chinese Peruvian. That's interesting. What part of Peru are you from?

B Vocabulary: Countries and nationalities

Study the words and phrases. Listen and repeat. Then try to add more countries and nationalities. 🔘 **Track 11**

Country	Brazil	Canada	Chile	China	Colombia	Costa Rica	Egypt
Nationality	Brazilian	Canadian	Chilean	Chinese	Colombian	Costa Rican	Egyptian
Country	Japan	Korea	Mexico	Peru	Spain	Thailand	the United States
Nationality	Japanese	Korean	Mexican	Peruvian	Spanish	Thai	American

Other countries: _____

Other nationalities: _____

C Common Questions and Answers

Study the words and phrases. Then practice with a partner.

Where are you from?
A: What part of (country name) are you from?
 = Where in _____ are you from?
B: I'm from _____.
A: What nationality are you?
B: I'm (nationality).

How do you spell that?
(Answer with letters of the alphabet.)

That's nice.
That's interesting.
That's a nice (noun).
That's an interesting _____.

D About You

Continue the visa application form.

Date of Birth (mm/dd/yyyy)	Nationality
_____	_____
Place of Birth	**Nationality at Birth**
_____	_____

Profession (Please list current position only.)
_____

Employer/Organization
_____

be questions with question words

question word + *be* + subject + ...	subject + *be* + ...
How are you today?	I'm very well, thanks.
Where is your boss from?	She's from Istanbul.
What is your last name?	It's Demir.
e?	We're in the classroom.
guys?	We're okay.
u **are** they from?	They're from Lima.

How...?

Where...?

vords in the box to make questions. Remember to

| is | are | you | where | are | you | how | it |

_____?   A: From Ankara, in Turkey.

_____?   A: Yes, I am.

_____?   A: Very well, thanks.

ountries. Try to label countries with English names that your

2. What countries did you label? Tell your teacher the nationalities of people from those countries.

3. Do you have any countries/nationalities that your classmates don't have? How many? _____

A   Model Conversation

Read the conversation. Then listen. 🔊 Track 12

Woman:	Hi. Aren't you Mr. Khalifa?
Man:	I am, yes. And you are…?
Kristina:	Kristina. I'm a new student. I'm in your class tomorrow.
Mr. Khalifa:	Tomorrow—the English for Academic Writing course, right?
Kristina:	Yep, that's the one. At 12 o'clock. Some of my friends are in there, too.
Mr. Khalifa:	Oh yeah? What are their names?
Kristina:	Tucker, Jameson, and Wyatt.
Mr. Khalifa:	Oh, those guys. I know them. They're very good students. Anyway, I have to be going. See you in tomorrow's class.
Kristina:	All right. Have a good day.
Mr. Khalifa:	You too.

> **Brief note**
> We say "anyway" to change the topic.

B   Vocabulary: Farewells

Study the expressions. Try to add more. Then practice with a partner.

At the end of class (teacher)		The farewell	Other farewells
That's all for today. We'll stop here.		See you (later / tomorrow / soon / then). Have a good morning / afternoon / day / night. Good night. Take care. Bye / Goodbye.	_____ _____ _____ _____ _____
Before a farewell			
I should…	…go.		
I have to…	…be going.		
I've got to…	…get going.		

C   In Your World

Fill in the blanks to complete the conversation. Then practice with a partner. Pretend it's the end of class.

(Teacher: That's all for today.)

You: All right. Well, I should _____. What _____ you?

Partner: Me too. See _____ _____.

You: Yep. Have a _____ _____.

★ **Change roles and practice again. Don't look at the book—look at your partner.**

D   Quick Review

Look back at the brief notes in this unit.

1. Where are the words? Write the lesson number. *aha* _____ *oh* _____ *hey* _____

2. Write 4 informal words: _____ _____ _____ _____

Grammar

Possessives

	singular	plural
	my	our
	your	your
	his / Jameson's	
	her / Miss Khalifa's	their / my friends'
	its / tomorrow's	

Grammar Practice

Look back at parts A and E. Fill in the blanks with words or letters from the box to complete the table.

's   class   her   friends   class   s'   names   's   their   's   his   its

name + -'s / -s'	possessive adjective	noun
1. Kristina _____	**2.** _____	**3.** _____
4. my friend _____	**5.** _____	**6.** _____
7. Mr. Khalifa _____	**8.** _____	**9.** _____
10. tomorrow _____	**11.** _____	**12.** _____

Use the Language

Farewells

Talk to a partner. Describe the situations in the pictures.

What farewells do the people use? Write.

1. The woman: _____

2. The father: _____

3. The mechanic: _____

Read to Speak

English speakers sometimes say *goodbye* using words from other languages. On the Internet, find three of these goodbyes. Write the words below.

_____   _____   _____

Pick one of these words. Find classmates who have the same word. Form a group and explain the word to your class. What language is it from? What does it mean?

A Chatting

Read the chat and answer the questions below.

1. What's the name of the student who takes a Spanish class? _____

2. Who's from Honduras? _____

3. When are they meeting? _____

B Write a Chat

Chat with a partner. Use language from the unit to describe yourself, a friend, a classmate, or a teacher. Use your phone or write on a separate piece of paper. Then copy it here.

C Reminder

Some Module 1 Goals in Unit 1

Put a check mark (✓) next to the things you can do.

_____ Understand and use basic introductions, greetings, and farewells

_____ Ask and answer simple personal questions; describe yourself simply

_____ Ask and answer basic questions

A Read to Speak

Read the list of popular baby names from 2016.* Listen to their pronunciations. Then choose ten names and look up their meanings. Which name is your favorite? 🎧 Track 13

Rank	Boy	Meaning	Girl	Meaning
1	Noah		Emma	
2	Liam		Olivia	
3	Ethan		Ava	
4	Mason		Sophia	
5	Lucas		Isabella	
6	Oliver		Mia	
7	Aiden		Charlotte	
8	Logan		Harper	
9	Elijah		Abigail	
10	James		Amelia	
11	Benjamin		Emily	
12	Jacob		Madison	
13	Jack		Avery	
14	Jackson		Sofia	
15	Michael		Lily	
16	Alexander		Chloe	
17	William		Ella	
18	Luke		Aria	
19	Carter		Evelyn	
20	Gabriel		Scarlett	
21	Owen		Riley	
22	Daniel		Aubrey	
23	Matthew		Elizabeth	
24	Henry		Layla	
25	Grayson		Ellie	

* from *babycenter.com*

B Write to Speak

Who are some popular celebrities in your country? Write five names.

_____   _____

_____   _____

_____

C Now Speak

1. **Congratulations. You're a celebrity! Use the information above to choose a name for yourself.**

   What's your (first and last) name?

   _____

2. **You and your partner are celebrities. You meet at a party. Introduce yourselves to each other.**

3. **Stand up with your celebrity partner. Introduce him or her to the class.**

Lesson 1 — What do you have in here?

A Authentic Text: A shopping list

Read the list. Then listen. Match the pictures with the words on the list. 🔘 Track 14

Beginning-of-semester shopping list

Things I need:
a planner
a backpack
a pack of pens (4) and a pack of pencils (10)
4 notebooks
4 folders
highlighters—a yellow, a green, and an orange
a USB flash drive (8 GB)
an umbrella
some sticky notes

Vocabulary What's on the list?

B Vocabulary: Numbers

Study the words. Then practice with a partner.

0 zero	1 one	2 two	3 three	4 four	5 five	6 six	7 seven	8 eight	9 nine
10 ten	11 eleven	12 twelve	13 thirteen	14 fourteen	15 fifteen	16 sixteen	17 seventeen	18 eighteen	19 nineteen
20 twenty	21 twenty-one	22 twenty-two	23 twenty-three	24 twenty-four	25 twenty-five	26 twenty-six	27 twenty-seven	28 twenty-eight	29 twenty-nine

30 thirty
40 forty
50 fifty
60 sixty
70 seventy
80 eighty
90 ninety
100 one hundred
1000 one thousand

C Listen and repeat. 🔘 Track 15

1. 13 (thirteen), 30 (thirty)
2. 14 (fourteen), 40 (forty)
3. 15 (fifteen), 50 (fifty)
4. 16 (sixteen), 60 (sixty)
5. 17 (seventeen), 70 (seventy)
6. 18 (eighteen), 80 (eighty)
7. 19 (nineteen), 90 (ninety)

D Practice with your partner. Take turns. Say a number from part C. Your partner writes it. Is it correct?

E Say the numbers. Then listen. 🔘 Track 16

1. 60
2. 200
3. 430%
4. 13
5. 47

F In Your World

Fill in the blanks with numbers and names of things.

What's in your classroom?   I see _____ _____, _____ _____, and

_____ _____.

Articles *a* and *an*

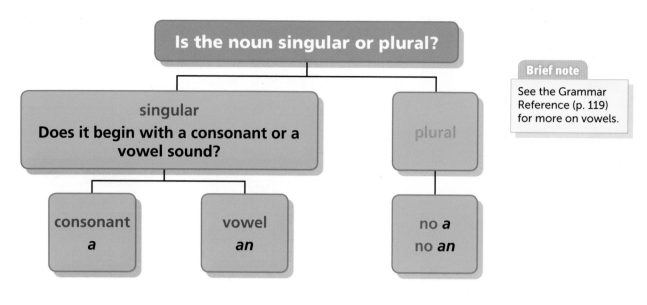

Brief note

See the Grammar Reference (p. 119) for more on vowels.

H **Grammar Practice**

Brief note

This *-s* means the noun is plural.

1. **Write *a*, *an*, or *x*.**

   a. ____ articles   b. ____ vowel   c. ____ consonant   d. ____ number   e. ____ boards
   f. ____ opposite   g. ____ boys   h. ____ name   i. ____ woman   j. ____ Australian

2. **Fill in the blanks with the words from the box.**

egg	item	language	staple

   k. an _____   l. a _____   m. a _____   n. an _____

I **Use the Language**

Brief note

See Lesson 2 (next 2 pages) for more information about *have* and *has*.

Making lists

List 1: Ask a partner about his or her items and list them below.

Do you have a notebook?
Do you have a(n) ____?
Do you have ____s? How many?

List 2: Choose a second partner. Listen to information about his or her first partner and write.

My partner has a notebook.
He has a(n) ____.
She has ten ____s.

_____

_____

_____

_____

_____

_____

_____

_____

A Authentic Text: A survey question

Read the instructions and fill out the survey form. Then discuss the questions below.

What do you have? Put a check mark (✓) next to all that apply.	☐ a girlfriend	☐ a dog
	☐ a boyfriend	☐ a cat
	☐ a bicycle	☐ a game console
	☐ a car	☐ a laptop computer
	☐ an airplane	☐ a tablet computer
	☐ a bus card	☐ a desktop computer

1. Talk about what you have with a partner.

2. What does "put a check mark next to all that apply" mean?

B Vocabulary

Look at the pictures. Fill in the blanks with vocabulary from the survey.

C About You

Make a list of what you have. Don't use words from above.

Grammar

Simple present: *have*

have questions and answers		*have* statements
Do I / you / we / they **have** a car?	✓ Yes, I do. (Yep, Yeah) ✗ No, I don't. (Nope)	I **have** a car. I **don't have** a car.
Does he / she / it **have** a computer?	✓ Yeah, it does. ✗ Nope.	It **has** a computer. It **doesn't have** a computer.

> **Brief note**
>
> Remember to use an article with a singular noun or -*s* with a plural one.

Grammar Practice

Fill in the blanks with words or letters from the box. Remember to capitalize.

has	are	does	yes	s	do	a	nope	an

1. Q: _____ she have a backpack?   A: Yeah, she does. She _____ three backpack___.

2. Q: _____ you have a list?   A: _____.

3. Q: _____ you __ student?   A: _____. I have _____ English class.

Fill in the blanks and circle the correct answers. Then practice the conversation with a partner.

4. **Man:** ❶ _____ you have a dog?

   Woman: Yeah, I ❷ (do / have). I ❸ _____ a brown one. His name's Georgie. I love him.

   Man: I ❹ (have / don't have) one, but I really ❺ (have / want) one.

5. **Woman:** I'm a really lucky girl. I ❶ _____ a great friend.

   Man: Oh, yeah? ❷ (What's her name / Where is she)?

   Woman: It's a guy, actually. His name is Marco. He's Italian.

   Man: Oh, cool. Yeah, you're lucky to ❸ (be / have) a good friend.

Use the Language

Writing about your things

Look back at part C. Choose 4 things you have. Write two sentences about each one.

1. I have _____. It's _____.

2. _____

3. _____

4. _____

A Authentic Text: A descriptive paragraph

Read the paragraph. Then listen. ⏵ Track 17

My Backpack

My backpack is special because it's very colorful. It's yellow, pink, red, and blue. Right now it's really full. There's an apple in it. The apple is mine. Some other stuff in it isn't mine. There are four colorful pens in it. They're my classmate Juanita's. The orange and red notebook is hers, too. I have a brother, Mike. The tablet in my backpack is ours. We don't have two tablets because tablets are expensive. Anyway, that's my backpack. Tell me about yours.

B About You

Write a descriptive paragraph about something that's yours.

_____

_____

_____

_____

C Vocabulary: Colors

Brief note
You saw yellow, green, and orange in Unit 2 Lesson 1.

Study the words. Then listen and repeat. ⏵ Track 18

red	yellow	blue	green
purple	pink	orange	magenta
gray	black	white	brown

D In Your World

Brief note
Answer with a possessive adjective or a noun ending with -'s / -s'. Look back at Unit 1 Lesson 5 OR preview the next page and answer with a possessive pronoun.

Talk to your partner about what you see. Use these questions and statements:

What do you see?   I see a(n) _____.   I see _____.

What color is it?   What color are they?   Whose is it?   Whose are they?

E Grammar

Brief note

For *it*, don't use a possessive **pronoun**. Use the noun.
Q: Whose bowl is it?
✓ A: The dog's.   ✗ A: Its.

Possessives: pronouns and questions

questions				possessives	
Whose	**noun**	*is/are*	**pronoun**	Mine. Yours. Hers. / His. The teacher's.	Ours. Yours. [*plural*] Theirs. The students'. Mike and Lisa's.
Whose	backpack	is	it?		
	tablets	are	they?		

F Grammar Practice

Fill in the blanks with a word, an *s*, or an *'s*.

1. Q: _____ egg is it?   A: It's your egg. It's _____.

2. Q: Is Julia_____ backpack red?   A: Yes, _____ has a red backpack.

3. Q: Is it _____ pencil?   A: Yes, _____ mine. _____ eraser is yellow.

4. Q: Whose pencil _____ she have? A: She _____ her pencil. It's _____.

Put the words in order to make (1) a question and (2) a statement. Use one capital letter in the question and one in the statement.

theirs / is / it   (1) _____?   A: Yes, it is.

                     (2) _____.

G Use the Language

Brief note

Take notes means write things you see or hear.

Talking about your things

Talk with your partner about things you have and things your partner has. Use vocabulary and grammar from Lessons 1, 2, and 3. Take notes.

Partner _____   Me _____

_____   _____

_____   _____

Remember and write things from your conversation. Circle the speaker.

Brief note

The *speaker* is the person who talks.

Me / Partner: _____

Me / Partner: _____

Me / Partner: _____

Me / Partner: _____

Me / Partner: _____

A   Authentic Text: Labeled pictures

Study the labels. Then listen. `Track 19`

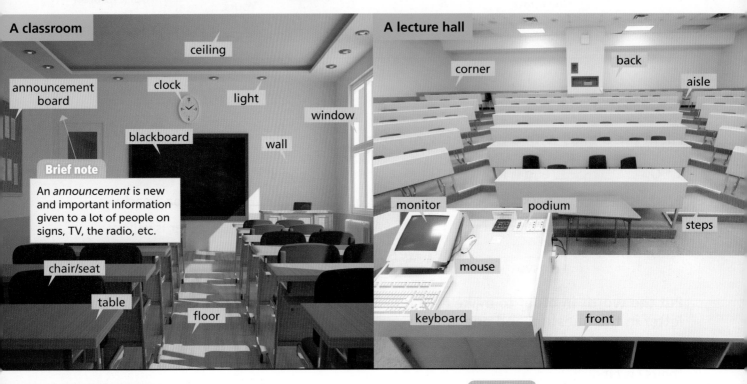

A classroom

ceiling

announcement board

clock

light

window

blackboard

wall

Brief note

An *announcement* is new and important information given to a lot of people on signs, TV, the radio, etc.

chair/seat

table

floor

A lecture hall

corner

back

aisle

monitor

podium

steps

mouse

keyboard

front

B   Listening

Brief note

Look at the words *chair* and *seat*. Ask your teacher about the word *sit*.

Description of a room `Track 20`

Listen to the description of a room. Is it the classroom on the left or the right? _____

C   In Your World

1. Look around your classroom. Ask your teacher about things. Say, "What do you call this in English?"

2. What's in your classroom? Using the labels above and your teacher's answers, make a list.

Things in my classroom

D Grammar

Questions and statements with *there is* and *there are*

singular noun	plural noun
Is there a clock? **There is** a clock.	**Are there** clocks? **There are** clocks.

Brief note

Notice the difference between *their, there,* and *they're*. Explain the difference to your teacher.

E Grammar Practice

Fill in the blanks with *is, are, a, an,* or *x*.

1. There _____ _____ umbrella.

2. There _____ _____ Australians.

3. There _____ _____ question.

4. There _____ _____ questions.

5. There _____ _____ answers.

6. There _____ _____ egg.

7. There _____ _____ chair.

8. There _____ _____ case.

9. There _____ _____ eggs.

10. There _____ _____ paragraph.

Circle the correct answers.

11. (There / Are) you a student?

12. (There / You) is a chair.

13. There (is / am) a student.

14. Your teacher (is / there is) in his chair.

15. (Are / There are) you a teacher?

16. (There is / There are) eggs in my pencil case.

17. (There is / Is there) a folder on my desk.

18. (There is / Is there) a folder on my desk?

19. (Are / There) there pens and pencils?

20. Yes, (there / you) are.

F Prewrite

Fill in the blanks with *is* or *are* and a noun. Add an article for singular nouns and an *-s* for plural nouns. Use numbers, too.

1. In my university classroom, there _____.

2. On my desk, there _____.

3. On the wall, there _____.

4. There _____ also _____.

G Use the Language

Writing descriptive paragraphs

Write a short descriptive paragraph about your classroom.

_____

_____

_____

_____

A Text Markup

Read the paragraph. Then follow the instructions below.

Describing My Classroom

Now I'm in my classroom. I see things. I see things I have. I see things my classmates have. I see things my teacher has. My things are on my desk. My English book is on my desk. My pens and pencils are next to it. There is one pencil. The pencil is on the right side of the book. There are three pens on the book's left side. A blue pen is between two black pens. The backpack under my chair is mine, too. My pencil case, dictionary, and folder are inside it. I don't see them. I see my classmates' desks around me. My teacher's things are in front of me. The big desk is hers. On it, there is a computer. It's hers, too. Her chair is behind the desk, and the board is behind the chair. Of course, there are also walls, a floor, and a ceiling in the room. I am between the ceiling and the floor, and the walls are around me.

1. Underline the articles one time.
2. Put a star (*) on the right side of the *have* verbs.
3. Underline the possessive pronouns two times.
4. Put a square around every *there is* or *there are*.

> **Brief note**
> "Of course" means something is natural or expected.

B Vocabulary: Prepositions of location

Listen. Use your hands to practice as you repeat. 🔴 Track 21

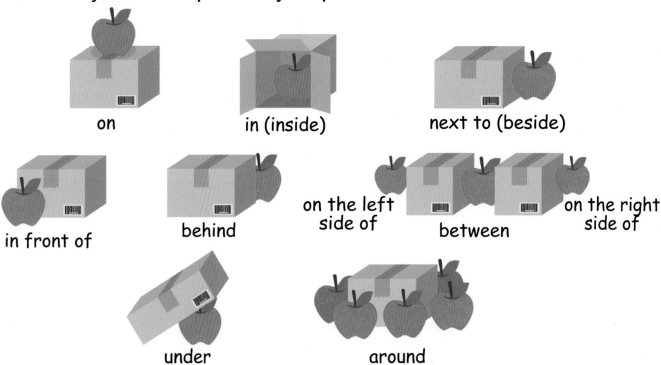

on

in (inside)

next to (beside)

in front of

behind

on the left side of

between

on the right side of

under

around

Now circle the prepositions in the paragraph above.

C In Your World

Talk to your partner about what you see. Use these questions:

What do you see?   Where is it?

Brief note

The noun after the preposition is called the preposition's object.

D Grammar

Prepositions of location and prepositional phrases

Prepositions of location tell where things are. They often come after the verb *be* and before a noun.

My <u>backpack</u> **is** <u>under</u> the <u>chair</u>.
  subject *be* prep.   noun

A preposition + noun is called a prepositional phrase. Prepositional phrases tell where the subject is. With no noun after the preposition, you don't know where the subject is.

My pencil is in a _____.

Where is the pencil? Do you know?

Between the preposition and the noun, you often see an article or a possessive adjective.

on **a** wall   in **my** backpack

Two (or more) nouns come after the preposition *between*.

Brief note

The "two nouns" after *between* can be one plural noun. For example, *between the chairs*.

The blue <u>pen</u> is **between** the red <u>pen</u> **and** the white <u>pen</u>.
      n.   n. *AND*   n.

The book is **between** the pens. (Plural -s means more than one pen.)

E Grammar Practice

Circle the correct phrases and sentences. Put an *X* on the left side of the wrong ones. Then rewrite them correctly.

1. between the desk _____
2. between desks _____
3. on floor _____
4. on the floor _____
5. My pencil is in. _____

6. An egg is in be. _____
7. It's in my hand. _____
8. It's in my desk. _____
9. My classmate is next to me.
_____

F Use the Language

Talking about your environment

Write sentences about your classroom or campus. Use prepositional phrases.

_____   _____

_____   _____

_____   _____

_____   _____

_____   _____

Find a partner. Don't show your sentences to your partner. Read only the prepositional phrases. Your partner has to guess the subject of your sentence. It's okay for your partner to ask questions.

Notes

Prof. Keats is sick at home. He writes a note to ask his neighbor Mia to get some of his things from work. Read the note.

Hi, Mia.

Thank you so much for doing this. I really have to grade these papers, but I can't drive my car right now.

My office is Room 243 in the Business Building. You have the key, so you can unlock it. The light switch is on the wall on the right side of the door. On the desk, there is a laptop computer. Please bring it. There are two piles of students' notebooks on my desk. One is under a red pen. There are 13 notebooks. Please count them, and please bring all of them. Bring the pen too, please. Also, I have four folders on the floor on the left side of my chair. Please bring those, too. There is a backpack behind the chair next to the wall. You can use it to carry everything.

Mia, I have a small refrigerator on the floor next to the desk. There are drinks in it. Please have one. Thanks again for helping!

Fill in the blanks to make sentences about Prof. Keats's office. Use *have/has* or *there is/are*.

1. Prof. Keats _____ on his desk.

2. _____ on the floor of the office.

Write a Note

Pretend you are sick. Write a note. Describe how someone can do something for you.

_____

_____

_____

_____

_____

_____

Reminder

Some Module 1 Goals in Unit 2

Put a check mark (✓) next to the things you can do.

_____ Understand and use common classroom language

_____ Understand and use simple words in descriptions of objects (for example, colors)

_____ Understand and use numbers to count

Warm Up

Talk with your teacher or in a group. Ask and answer questions about your classroom. Try to use the vocabulary and grammar from the unit.

Listen for Information   🔊 Track 22

1. **Listen to a woman describe a classroom. Fill in the blanks or circle the correct answers.**

   a. _____ desks in the classroom

   b. _____ students in the class

   c. What is the teacher's title?
   (Miss / Mrs. / Mr.)

   d. _____ students in the room now

   e. What class? _____

   f. What word is on the board?
   (only / oily / hola)

2. **Listen again. Follow the instructions.**

   a. Draw the teacher.

   b. Circle Nancy's chair.

   c. Write *only*, *oily*, or *hola* on the board.

   d. Draw a purple book on Laura's desk.

   e. Draw a pen on Thomas's desk.

   f. Draw two apples on Larry's desk.

Discuss

1. Look at a partner's book. Is it the same or different?

2. Now show your teacher your work. Is it correct?

3. What's the difference between *in front of* and *at the front of*? Discuss with a partner or your teacher.

4. What's the difference between your classroom and the one above? Discuss with a partner or your teacher.

A Vocabulary

Remember and write...

1. ...five colors.

   _____ _____ _____ _____ _____

2. ...five prepositions.

   _____ _____ _____ _____ _____

3. ...three jobs and two titles.

   _____ _____ _____ _____ _____

4. ...three countries and the nationalities of people from there.

   _____ / _____ _____ / _____ _____ / _____

5. ...three things people can have in their backpacks. Then flip through the module and write two more.

   _____ _____ _____ _____ _____

6. ...three things people can have outside the classroom. Then flip through the module and write two more.

   _____ _____ _____ _____ _____

B Grammar

Look back at the module. Fill in the blanks.

1. _____ good to meet you.

2. Martín, _____ you the tutor?

3. Please _____ me Angela.

4. Angela _____ married.

5. Where are you _____, Biyu?

6. What are _____ names?

7. _____ a good day.

8. I'm in Mr. _____ class tomorrow.

9. I need _____ umbrella.

10. You need _____ backpack.

11. I _____ a boyfriend.

12. I _____ have a girlfriend.

13. _____ dog is he?

14. _____ are Chinese students in my class.

15. I sit in _____ of you.

16. You sit _____ me.

17. He sits next _____ me.

18. I sit between you _____ him.

C Introductions and the Classroom

1. Your partner is a new student. Introduce yourself and tell your partner about your class. Then answer his or her questions.

2. Now change. You are the new student. Ask your partner questions about your class.

D Guess the Statement

1. Write a true statement about your class—the room, your teacher, or a classmate.

    _____

2. Tell the class what your statement is about—the room, the teacher, a classmate, etc.

3. Now your classmates guess your statement.

E Put It Together

Write five sentences about the picture below.

1. _____

2. _____

3. _____

4. _____

5. _____

Module 2 Goals

Build a vocabulary of words and phrases about family and personal details

Describe your family in short, simple spoken or written phrases

Understand, ask, and answer simple personal questions such as *How old are you?*

Understand and use days of the week and months of the year

Understand and use numbers as ages and dates

Give personal information, such as age and basic information about family

Describe your family simply (for example, the members, how old they are, and what they do)

Indicate time by such phrases as *in November*

Preview

Look at pages 36 to 61. What pages are these things on?

plural spelling rules   _____

a family tree   _____

a woman practicing guitar   _____

the names of months   _____

Discuss

Talk about the questions with a partner.

1. Who do you think the people are?
   I think … are …

2. In your language, what word means *family*?
   In my …, the word … means family.

3. What family members do you have pictures of?
   I … of my … and my …

4. Who in your family is still in school or university?
   My … is still in …

5. What do students at your school or university do on the weekend?
   At my …, most students … on the weekend.

   _____

Lesson 1   In My Family

A   Model Conversation

Read the conversation. Then listen. 🔊 Track 23

Louis:	That's a nice bag.
Carmen:	Thanks. It's my brother's.
Louis:	Ah, you have a brother?
Carmen:	I have three brothers, actually.
Louis:	How many sisters do you have?
Carmen:	I don't have any sisters. I'm the only girl.
Louis:	You must be your mom and dad's favorite.
Carmen:	What about you? How many siblings do you have?
Louis:	Just one. My younger sister.

> **Brief note**
> We say "actually" to correct a previous statement.

> **Brief note**
> "Mom" and "dad" are less formal ways to say *mother* and *father*.

B   Vocabulary: Family members

Listen to the conversation again. Then fill in the blanks with vocabulary words. 🔊 Track 23

Carmen's family

Nicolas	Patricia	Andres	Samuel	Sebastian	Carmen
father	mother	brother	brother	brother	sister

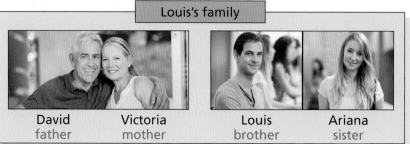

Louis's family

David	Victoria	Louis	Ariana
father	mother	brother	sister

1. Carmen doesn't have any _____.
2. She has an older _____ named Andres.
3. Her _____'s name is Patricia.
4. Louis has a younger _____ named Ariana.

C   In Your World

Write the names of some of your family members below. Then choose a partner. Tell your partner about your family. Write down the names of some of your partner's family members.

My family	My partner's family
_____	_____

D Grammar

how many questions and their answers

how many questions	answers to how many questions
How many brothers do you have? **How many** children do you have?	I have **three** brothers. I **don't** have **any** children.
How many siblings does Louis have?	He has **one** sibling.
How many people are there in your family?	There are **six** people in my family.

> **Brief note**
>
> See Unit 3 Lesson 2 to learn more about *any*.

E Grammar Practice

Put the words in order to make questions with *how many*. Then check the correct answers.

Questions

1. sisters / you / have / how / many / do

   _____?

2. how / children / many / do / you / have

   _____?

3. there / are / how / many / in / your / family / people

   _____?

Answers

☐ Yes, I have a sister.
☐ I have one sister.

☐ I have two children.
☐ I have some children.

☐ Four people.
☐ My family is small.

F Use the Language

Filling in a table

Talk about your family and your partner's family. Then fill in the boxes below.

_____'s family	
Name: Relationship: Other information:	Name: Relationship: Other information:
Name: Relationship: Other information:	Name: Relationship: Other information:
Name: Relationship: Other information:	Name: Relationship: Other information:

A Model Conversation

Read the conversation. Then listen. 🔊 Track 24

Gabriel: Korea is really far away. Do you miss your family?

Jihyun: I miss them, but I have some relatives here. And I talk to my family online.

Gabriel: Do you have any pictures of your family?

Jihyun: Yes. I have some on my phone. Just a second... Here.

Gabriel: Oh, your brother looks smart. What does he do?

Jihyun: He's a student. He studies computer science.

Brief note

"Just a second" means *wait*.

B Vocabulary: Technology and media

Brief note

A notebook computer is the same thing as a laptop computer.

Study the words. Then listen and repeat. 🔊 Track 25

phone

notebook computer

headphones

digital camera

online

picture

photo

selfie

C In Your World

Write the four pieces of technology from part B in the blanks below. Use an article if necessary. Put a check mark next to the ones that you have. Then choose a partner and ask which ones he or she has.

I have...

☐ _____

☐ _____

☐ _____

☐ _____

My partner has...

☐ _____

☐ _____

☐ _____

☐ _____

D Grammar

some and any

questions with *any*	answers	statements with *some* and *any*
Do you have **any** pictures of your family?	✓ Yes, I do. ✗ No, I don't.	✓ I have **some** pictures on my tablet. ✗ I don't have **any** pictures on my tablet.
Does she have **any** relatives here?	✓ Yes, she does. ✗ No, she doesn't.	✓ She has **some** relatives here. ✗ She doesn't have **any** relatives here.

E Grammar Practice

Is the grammar in these sentences correct or incorrect? Write *correct*, or underline the mistake and write the sentence correctly.

1. Do you have some brothers?

   _____

2. I have some pictures of my family.

   _____

3. He doesn't have any children.

   _____

4. I don't have some siblings.

   _____

5. Does he have some sisters?

   _____

F Listen to Speak

Listen to two conversations. Which conversation matches the picture? Who are the speakers in each conversation? 🔘 Track 26

Tell your partner. Does your partner agree? Why or why not? Write.

_____

_____

_____

_____

_____

_____

_____

Lesson 3 — Family Photos

A Model Conversation

Read the conversation. Then listen. 🔊 Track 27

Antoni: Do you have any pictures of your family on your computer?

Eisha: Umm. Well, here's one.

Antoni: Who is this next to the chair?

Eisha: That's my sister.

Antoni: Wow, she looks like you.

Eisha: A lot of people say that. Oh, and there's this one too.

Antoni: Who are they?

Eisha: They're my parents, and that's our dog.

> **Brief note**
> We say "umm" when we're thinking.

B Vocabulary: Demonstratives

Study the words. Then listen and repeat. 🔊 Track 28

this   that

these   those

> **Brief note**
> You can abbreviate *that is* to *that's*, but don't abbreviate the other demonstratives.

C Demonstratives in Conversation

Read. Then listen and repeat. 🔊 Track 29

"**This** is my sister."
"**That's** our chair."

"**These** are my parents."
"**That's** our dog."

Practice using *this*, *that*, *these*, and *those* with the classroom vocabulary from Unit 2.

D About You

Do you have a picture of a friend or family member?

Yes: Present the picture to your partner.

No: Choose one of the pictures from Modules 1 or 2. Pretend you know the people.

Use demonstrative pronouns to introduce the person or people in the picture.

Grammar

Questions with *who*

subject	question	answer
singular	**Who** is the person in this picture? **Who** is this next to the chair? **Who** is that?	This That ⎱ is my mom.
plural	**Who** are they? ~~**Who** are those?~~	These Those ⎱ are my parents. They

Grammar Practice

Use demonstrative pronouns to write *who* questions about each picture. Then think about answers. Practice asking and answering the questions with a partner.

1. Who _____?

3. Who _____?

2. Who _____?

4. Who _____?

Use the Language

Talking about photos

Choose a partner. Look at the first picture. Ask your partner about the picture. Who are the people? After your partner tells you, change roles and talk about the second picture.

So, who are the people in the pictures? Write a sentence about each person.

Picture 1: _____

Picture 2: _____

A   Model Conversation

Read the conversation. Then listen. 🔊 Track 30

Noah: Thanks for coming, Lili! How's the party?

Lili: It's very nice. Thank you for inviting me. Your family is interesting. Who are those women?

Noah: The two women with long brown hair? They're my cousins.

Lili: Oh, okay. Who is the older woman they're with? Their mom?

Noah: Right. My aunt. But her ex-husband isn't here. And the man at the table is my uncle.

Lili: Who are those women with him, holding those glasses?

Noah: They're his ex-wives. They're all friends.

B   Vocabulary: Extended family

Study the words. Then fill in the blanks below.

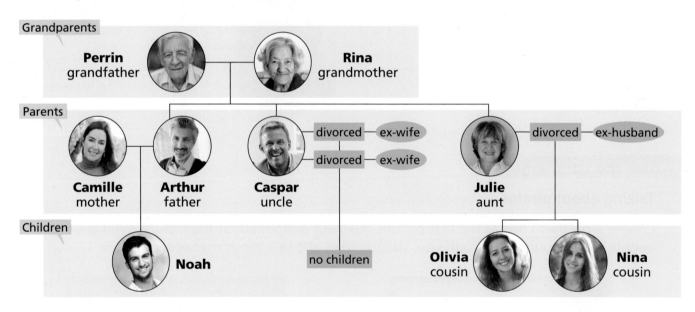

1. Noah has two _____, Nina and Olivia.
2. He only has one _____. Her name is Julie.
3. Julie's _____ is not at the party.
4. Caspar is Noah's ⓐ _____. He has two ⓑ _____.
5. Both Julie and Caspar are _____.
6. Noah's _____ are Perrin and Rina.

C   Demonstrative Adjectives

Listen and fill in the blanks with the demonstrative adjectives that you hear. 🔊 Track 31

demonstrative adjectives		
singular	**this** person	**that** person
plural	**these** people	**those** people

1. Who are _____ men?
2. Can I see _____ picture?

D   Grammar

Plurals

plural spellings		irregular plurals	
+s			
cousin	cousin**s**		
grandparent	grandparent**s**		
-x, -s, -ch, -sh → +es		child	**children**
box	box**es**		
glass	glass**es**	person	**people**
-y → +ies		man	**men**
family	famil**ies**		
baby	bab**ies**	woman	**women**
-fe → +ves			
ex-wife	ex-wi**ves**		
yourself	yoursel**ves**		

E   Grammar Practice

Fill in each blank with the plural form of the word in parentheses. Then listen and check your answers. ⊙ Track 32

1. Who are the women holding (glass) _____?

2. Do you have any (child) _____?

3. All of my (grandparent) _____ live nearby.

4. Caspar has two (ex-wife) _____.

5. I have more than 20 (cousin) _____.

6. Yuki just had twins—two (baby) _____ at once!

7. Several (family) _____ live in my neighborhood.

8. My teachers are all (woman) _____.

F   Listen to Speak

Listen to the man. Answer the questions. ⊙ Track 33

1. How many aunts does the man have?   _____

2. How many uncles does he have?   _____

G   Use the Language

Interviews

Using language from this unit and other (English) language you know, interview your partner about his or her extended family. Take notes on what your partner says. Then open your book and fill in the table below.

Relation	How many?	Names	Other details
Aunts			
Uncles			
Cousins			

A   Authentic Text: A descriptive paragraph

Read the paragraph. Then listen. Track 34

Hanging Out with Friends

These are my friends. Actually, the woman with long brown hair is my younger sister. She's 22 years old. That man next to her with that hat is her boyfriend. He's also my friend. This guy, with the beard and the gray T-shirt, is my friend Seth. He's an artist and a musician. The woman with short hair is another friend. I work with her at a university. We meet at this coffee shop to talk and laugh. It's always fun to hang out together.

Brief note

"Hang out" means spend time relaxing and having fun.

B   Comprehension

Listen again and fill in the blanks. Track 34

1. The man with _____ is an artist.
2. The woman with _____ hair is her sister.
3. The woman with _____ works with her.

C   Vocabulary: Appearance

Study the words and phrases. Then listen and repeat. Track 35

Hair	Color	blond	red	brown	black
	Length	long		short	
Facial hair		beard	goatee	mustache	
Height			short	tall	

D   In Your World

Work with a partner. Describe the appearance of one of your classmates.

E Grammar

Describing appearance using *with* prepositional phrases

Brief note

Notice when to use *a* and when to use *the*.

statement + *who* question	*who* question using *with*
A man has a beard. Who is the man? →	Who is the man **with a beard**?
A woman has red hair. Who is the woman? →	Who is the woman **with red hair**?
two statements	**one statement using *with***
A man has brown hair. He's my friend. →	The man **with brown hair** is my friend.
A woman has glasses. She's my mom. →	The woman **with glasses** is my mom.
simple description	**description using *with***
that man, the one who has long hair →	the man **with long hair**
there is	**there are**
There is a man **with a beard**.	There are women **with long hair**.

F Grammar Practice

Using the chart above, fill in the blanks.

1. that girl, the one who has blond hair   → _____

2. that man, the one who has a goatee   → _____

3. that teacher, the one who has black hair   → _____

G Write to Speak

Look at the picture below. Write a description.

_____

_____

H Use the Language

Describing a picture

1. Choose a picture from Units 1–3 of this book. Write the page number below.

   My picture is on page _____.

2. Remember what the people in that picture look like. Then close your book.

3. Choose a partner and describe the picture. Your partner flips through the book and guesses the page that the picture is on.

4. Now change roles. Try to guess which picture your partner is describing. Write the page number below.

   My partner's picture is on page

   _____.

A Family Tree

Read Jason's family tree and answer the questions.

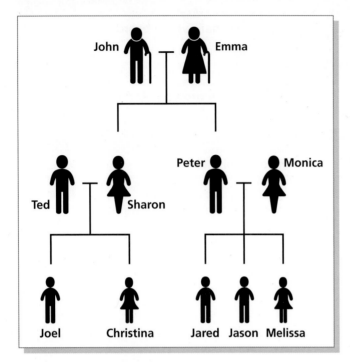

1. Circle Jason.

2. John is Jason's

   _____.

3. Who is Jason's aunt?

   _____

4. What are the names of Jason's siblings?

   _____

5. How many cousins does Jason have?

   _____

B Draw a Family Tree

Now draw your own family tree. Tell your partner about each person. Are they single, married, or divorced? What do they do?

My Family

C Reminder

Some Module 2 Goals in Unit 3

Put a check mark (✓) next to the things you can do.

_____ Build a vocabulary of words and phrases about family and personal details

_____ Describe your family in short, simple spoken or written phrases

_____ Give personal information, such as age and basic information about family

Read to Write

Read Jason's paragraph about his family.

My Family

My parents' names are Monica and Peter. My dad, Peter, is an accountant. My mom, Monica, is a teacher. I have two siblings. Jared is my older brother. He is 25 years old, and he works as an engineer. He isn't married, but he has a girlfriend. My younger sister's name is Melissa. She's 19, and she's still a student, so she isn't married. She's in college, studying business.

Prewrite

Prepare to write by answering the questions.

Question	My answers
What are your parents' names?	
What does your father do?	
What does your mother do?	
How many siblings do you have?	
What are their names?	
How old are they?	
What do they do?	
Are they married?	

Now Write

Write a short paragraph about your family. Write everything you can write in three minutes. Then stop.

_____

_____

_____

_____

_____

_____

Read your paragraph to the class. Listen to your classmates. Whose paragraph is the longest?

★ Unit 4 · School Life ★

Lesson 1 Ages and Birthdays

A Model Conversation

Read the conversation. Then listen. 🔊 Track 36

Fuad: Hey, you two. How are you doing?

Salma: Well, I'm great. Today's my birthday!

Fuad: Oh, really?

Salma: Yeah, April 23rd.

Fuad: Well, happy birthday! How old are you?

Salma: I'm 21.

Fuad: Cool! Do you have any special plans?

Salma: Nope, just a family party. When's your birthday, Fuad?

Fuad: It's on October 14th. It's a long time from now.

> **Brief note**
> "Cool" often means nice, good, or okay.

B Vocabulary: Dates

Study the words. Then listen to the dates below and practice. 🔊 Track 37

Months	Dates (1st–19th)
January	- Except for 1, 2, and 3, add -th.
February	- Sometimes the spelling changes.
March	**1** first 11 eleventh
April	**2** second 12 twelfth
May	**3** third 13 thirteenth
June	4 fourth 14 fourteenth
July	5 fifth 15 fifteenth
August	6 sixth 16 sixteenth
September	7 seventh 17 seventeenth
October	8 eighth 18 eighteenth
November	9 ninth 19 nineteenth
December	10 tenth

Dates (20th and 30th)
(change -y to -i and add -eth)
20 twentieth
30 thirtieth

Dates (21st–29th & 31st)
(say "twenty" or "thirty" and the ordinal number)
21 twenty-first
22 twenty-second
...
31 thirty-first

1. January 21st
2. October 18th

3. June 13th
4. March 26th

5. November 11th
6. August 2nd

C Ordinal Numbers

Change the numbers to ordinals. Some are done for you.

one	→ first	two	→ _____	three	→ third
nine	→ _____	twelve	→ _____	seventeen	→ _____
twenty	→ _____	twenty-six	→ twenty-sixth	thirty-one	→ _____

D About You

Write your birthday below. Then choose a partner. Tell him or her when your birthday is. Ask when your partner's birthday is.

My birthday: _____   My partner's birthday: _____

Grammar

Questions with *when* and *how old*

question word(s)	*be* verb	subject	answer
When	is	your birthday? the party?	It's on the 23rd. It's on October 14th.
How old	are is	you? your dad?	I'm 21. He's 65 years old.

questions with when and how old + be

Grammar Practice

Choose the correct answers. Then listen and check. 🔊 Track 38

Questions

1. When is your mom's birthday?

2. How old is your brother?

3. When is the test?

4. How old are you?

Answers

☐ It's on the eighteenth.
☐ It's on eighteen.

☐ He's twenty-nine.
☐ He's twenty-ninth.

☐ It's on the three.
☐ It's on the third.

☐ I'm 20 years.
☐ I'm 20 years old.

Use the Language

Invitations

Make a birthday party invitation. Write the date of the party, the date of your birthday, and your age on the invitation. Add other information, too. Use the Internet for ideas. Show the invitation to your classmates, and invite them to the party. Fill in the table with classmates' names, birthdays, and ages.

INVITATIONS		
Classmate's name	Birthday	Age

A Model Conversation

Read the conversation. Then listen. Track 39

Maria: Do you have an English class this semester, Sabrina?
Sabrina: Yes, I do. I learn a lot in that class.
Maria: What do you do in there?
Sabrina: Normal things, really. We learn new grammar and vocabulary, and we practice speaking all the time.
Maria: Do you read a lot?
Sabrina: No, not that much. But I take a lot of notes, and we discuss interesting topics. How's your Arabic class?
Maria: It's difficult, but good. It's a beginner class. We write Arabic letters and learn to read new words.
Sabrina: Whoa. That sounds hard.

Brief note
We say "whoa" when we're surprised.

B Vocabulary

Listen to the conversation again. Then fill in the blanks with vocabulary words or phrases.
Track 39

 study	 read	 write	 learn
 discuss	 take notes	 practice	 take a test

1. We **a** _____ new grammar and vocabulary, and we **b** _____ speaking all the time.
2. I **a** _____ a lot of **b** _____, and we **c** _____ interesting topics.
3. We **a** _____ a hundred new letters every week. I **b** _____ a lot.

C About You

Check off the activities that you do every day. Exchange information with a partner.

You: *I practice English every day. What about you?*
Your partner: *I practice it every day, too.*

Brief note
When you and your partner do the same thing, say "too" at the end of the sentence.

☐ practice English   ☐ take notes
☐ learn something new   ☐ write emails
☐ discuss interesting topics ☐ read the news

D Grammar

Simple present in affirmative statements

singular subject			plural subject		
subject	verb	more information	subject	verb	more information
I	**take** **write**	notes. stories.	We	**discuss**	interesting topics.
You	**practice** **learn**	often. quickly.	You (guys/all)	**read** **study**	well. hard.
			They	**take**	a test every month.

Brief note

See Unit 4 Lesson 4 to learn about statements with *he*, *she*, and *it*.

E Grammar Practice

Use the words in the box to make statements. Use each word once. Then make a statement without using the verbs in the box. (Hint: Check other lessons. For example, in Unit 4 Lesson 1, there are *make*, *show*, *invite*, etc.)

notes	they	speaking	I	take	learn	we	grammar	practice

1. _____
(words from the box)

2. _____
(words from the box)

3. _____
(words from the box)

4. _____
(verb not in box)

F Use the Language

Good study habits

Look at the list of good study habits. Add to the list, and put a check mark next to those that you do. Then interview a partner and put a check mark next to the habits that your partner does.

Brief note

A *habit* is something that you do often.

		Good Study Habits
Me	**My partner**	**Habit**
____	____	take notes in every class
____	____	read everything again after class
____	____	write a list of the things you need to learn
____	____	practice all the time
____	____	
____	____	
____	____	
____	____	
____	____	
____	____	

Lesson 3 — Do you have class on Friday?

A Authentic Text: A planner

Read the weekly planner.

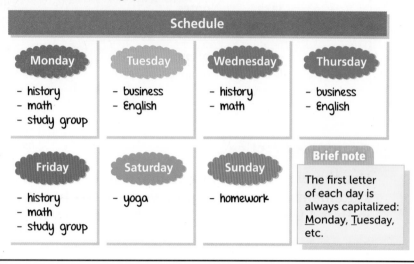

Schedule

Monday
- history
- math
- study group

Tuesday
- business
- English

Wednesday
- history
- math

Thursday
- business
- English

Friday
- history
- math
- study group

Saturday
- yoga

Sunday
- homework

Brief note
The first letter of each day is always capitalized: Monday, Tuesday, etc.

B Vocabulary: Days of the week

Study the words and abbreviations. Then listen and repeat. Track 40

MONDAY	TUESDAY	WEDNESDAY	THURSDAY	FRIDAY	SATURDAY	SUNDAY
MON	**TUE**	**WED**	**THU**	**FRI**	**SAT**	**SUN**

C Vocabulary: Words with *week*

Study the words and phrases. Then fill in the blanks below.

Weekdays — MON TUE WED THU FRI **Weekend** — SAT SUN **Workweek** — MON TUE WED THU FRI

1. The ⓐ _____ starts on Monday and ends on ⓑ _____.

2. Monday is a ⓐ _____, but Saturday isn't.

3. Saturday and ⓐ _____ are the ⓑ _____.

Brief note
To talk about the same day of every week, you can make the *-day* plural: *I like Tuesdays.*

D In Your World

Choose a partner. Ask and answer the questions below. Then write your partner's answers.

Q: What day of the week do you like most? What do you do on that day?

_____

_____

Grammar

Simple present questions and answers

simple present questions				answers
Do/Does	subject	main verb	more information	
Do	I you we you [*plural*] they	**need** **have** **have** **need** **take**	a better grade? class on Friday? a test tomorrow? some help? notes in class?	Yes, you **do**. / No, you **don't**. Yes, I **do**. / No, I **don't**. Yes, you **do**. / No, you **don't**. Yes, we **do**. / No, we **don't**. Yes, they **do**. / No, they **don't**.
Does	she he	**study** **work**	on weekends? on Thursday?	Yes, she **does**. / No, she **doesn't**. Yes, he **does**. / No, he **doesn't**.

Grammar Practice

Change the simple present statements into simple present questions.

1. Sarah studies every weekend.

   _____?

2. Esteban goes to parties on Saturday.

   _____?

3. We take a quiz every Monday.

   _____?

4. I have class on Friday.

   _____?

Use the Language

Filling out a schedule

Work with a partner. Fill out the weekly schedule with your partner's information.

MON	
TUE	
WED	
THU	
FRI	
SAT	
SUN	

A Model Conversation

Read the conversation. Then listen. Track 41

Davi: So, do both of your brothers go to college too?

Isabel: No, my younger brother goes to high school. He's a senior. My older brother works for a tech company. He's a software engineer.

Davi: Oh, that's cool.

Isabel: What about your family? How many siblings do you have?

Davi: I have two older sisters. Alice goes to this university, actually. She's a senior.

Isabel: Oh. What does she study?

Davi: Math. And she plays sports here, too.

Isabel: Nice.

Davi: Yeah, and Giovanna is a tutor. But she also attends university part-time.

> **Brief note**
> Many people use *university* and *college* to mean the same thing. Ask your teacher about the differences.

B Vocabulary: School & grade levels

Study the words. Then listen and fill in the blanks. Track 42

Levels in School (United States)						
pre-K/ preschool	kindergarten	elementary school	middle school	high school		college/ university
		1st grade				
		2nd grade		9th grade / freshman		freshman
		3rd grade	7th grade	10th grade / sophomore		sophomore
		4th grade	8th grade	11th grade / junior		junior
		5th grade		12th grade / senior		senior
		6th grade				

1. Markus is a _____ in university.
2. Seohyeon is a _____ in high school.
3. Valentina is a _____ in college.
4. Elizabeth is in _____ _____ in elementary school.

C About You

Choose a partner. Tell her or him what year you are in or your job. Then think of a family member or relative and give the same information.

> **Brief note**
> Use *in* with grades and *a* or *an* with other nouns.

I'm a(n) / in _____ at _____.
　　　　　　(job, year, or grade)　　　　(company, university, high school name)

My _____ is a(n) / in _____ at _____.
　　(family member)　　　　(job, year, or grade)　　(company, university, high school name)

Grammar

Brief note

Look back at p. 43. Verbs with 3rd person singular subjects follow the same spelling rules as plural nouns.

Simple present in affirmative statements

3rd person singular subjects	other subjects
My older brother **works** for a tech company.	I **work** for a tech company.
Alice **goes** to this university.	You **go** out on weekends.
It **sounds** difficult.	
She **plays** sports here, too.	We **study** a lot.
Giovanna also **attends** university part-time.	They **play** soccer a lot.

Grammar Practice

Are the sentences correct or incorrect? Write correct, or underline the mistake and write the sentence correctly.

1. He go to this university.

_____

2. My sister studies biology.

_____

3. Jonathan are a doctor.

_____

4. She work for a finance company.

_____

Use the Language

Giving personal details

1. Listen to a student introducing Jihoon. Write the missing information. 🔊 Track 43

Jihoon	
Year/Grade	
Age	19
Major	
Other information	- from Korea - on weekends, goes out with friends, reads, and _____

2. Talk to a partner. Write information about them in the *My partner* table. Then choose another classmate and exchange information about your partners.

My partner: _____	

My classmate's partner: _____	

A   Model Conversation

Read the conversation. Then listen. 🎧 Track 44

Marisa: So, most of your classes are in the morning.

Bhavin: Actually, all of them are.

Marisa: Then what do you do in the afternoon?

Bhavin: Well, I have a lot of homework. I'm really busy this month. I have a big test on the 21ˢᵗ.

Marisa: Don't you ever go out?

Bhavin: Nope. I study at night, too. And on Friday, I plan my homework schedule for the weekend. On Saturday and Sunday, I study even more.

Marisa: Wow.

Bhavin: How about you? Don't you study?

Marisa: Of course I do. But mostly in December and May, before exams.

> **Brief note**
> We say "wow" when we're surprised.

B   Vocabulary: Times of day

Study the phrases. Then listen and repeat. 🎧 Track 45

| in the morning | in the afternoon | in the evening | at night |

C   Vocabulary: Daily activities

Study the words and phrases. For each activity, write the time of day when it is usually done. Use the times of day from part B.

| go out | get ready | have lunch | wake up |

_____   _____   _____   _____

| go to class | go to bed | go home | have dinner |

_____   _____   _____   _____

D   Quick Review

Look back at the brief notes in this module.

1. What word or phrase means... "nice"? _____ "wait"? _____

2. A *habit* is something that you do _____.

E   Grammar

Prepositional phrases of time

time of day	days & dates
in	*on*
I have class **in the morning**.	I exercise **on Monday, Wednesday,** and **Friday**.
She works **in the afternoon**.	Sofia studies **on Saturday**.
We have dinner together **in the evening**.	We always have quizzes **on Monday**.
at	The party is **on the 16th**.
Alejandro goes out **at night**.	The test is **on Friday, December 21st**.
day + time of day	months & seasons
on	*in*
I have math class **on Monday morning**.	I study hard **in December**.
I do all my homework **on Sunday night**.	Classes start **in January**.
She always does yoga **on Saturday afternoon**.	Every year, we visit Japan **in the summer**.

F   Grammar Practice

Write the correct preposition in each blank. Then check your answers with a partner.

1. Most of my classes are _____ the morning.
2. The school year starts _____ August.
3. I usually read _____ Sunday morning.
4. I don't go out _____ night.

5. Classes end _____ May.
6. We practice speaking _____ Wednesday.
7. The picnic is _____ Saturday.
8. I meet friends _____ Friday night.

G   Use the Language

Summarizing a schedule

Write your schedule for a normal weekday. Then write one for a normal Sunday.

My Normal Weekday
Morning
_____
_____
Afternoon
_____
_____
Evening
_____
_____

My Normal Sunday
Morning
_____
_____
Afternoon
_____
_____
Evening
_____
_____

Choose one of the schedules. Briefly tell your class about it.

A Surprise Party

Hana's birthday is soon. Her friend Chris writes a note to their friend Alicia to invite her to Hana's party. Read the note and answer the questions. Use complete sentences.

Hi Alicia,

   You know, Hana's birthday is on May 12ᵗʰ. That's this Saturday. It's a special birthday. She's a freshman, so it's her first birthday at university! She's only 18! I want to have a surprise party for her. She always practices violin on Saturday afternoon, so the party is in the evening. Do you want to come?

Chris

1. When is Hana's birthday? _____
2. When is the party? _____
3. How old is Hana? _____
4. What year is Hana in university? _____

Plan a surprise party for your friend or classmate. Work with a partner to answer questions about the person.

1. When is her/his birthday? _____
2. What day and time is the party? _____
3. How old is she/he? _____

B Write an Invitation

Following Chris's example, write a note. Invite people to your surprise party.

C Reminder

Some Module 2 Goals in Unit 4

Put a check mark (✓) next to the things you can do.

_____ Understand and use days of the week and months of the year

_____ Understand and use numbers as ages and dates

_____ Indicate time by such phrases as *in November*

A Listen for Information

Listen to the description of Brad Pitt. Then fill in the blanks. Track 46

1. He's an _____ man.

2. He's around _____ years old.

3. He has _____ hair.

4. His hair is usually _____.

5. Sometimes he has a _____.

6. He's _____.

B Brainstorm

Think of two celebrities. Don't write their names. Write three sentences to describe each of them.

1. _____

2. _____

3. _____

1. _____

2. _____

3. _____

C Organize

Listen to the description of Brad Pitt again. Number the details in the order that you hear them. Then write the same details about one of your celebrities. Track 46

#	Detail	My Celebrity	#	Detail	My Celebrity
____	Hair color	_____	____	Hair length	_____
____	Facial hair	_____	____	Marital status	_____
1	Nationality	_____	____	Age	_____

D Present

Describe your celebrity to the class. Don't say his or her name.

When a **classmate** presents, ask questions. Then guess the celebrity.

When **you** present, answer your classmates' questions.

A Vocabulary

Remember and write...

1. ...five family members.

_____ _____ _____ _____ _____

2. ...four technology or media devices.

_____ _____ _____ _____

3. ...four demonstrative pronouns.

_____ _____ _____ _____

4. ...five months of the year.

_____ _____ _____ _____ _____

5. ...two years of university. Then flip through the module, if necessary, and write the other two.

_____ _____ _____ _____

6. ...three activities people do at school. Then flip through the module, if necessary, and write two more.

_____ _____ _____ _____

B Grammar

Look back at the module. Fill in the blanks.

1. How _____ sisters do you have?

2. I _____ three brothers.

3. Do you have _____ pictures of your family?

4. She doesn't have _____ relatives here.

5. Who is _____ next to the chair?

6. Caspar has two _____ .

7. My teachers are all _____ .

8. Who is the woman _____ red hair?

9. _____ 's the party?

10. The man _____ brown hair is my friend.

11. He's 65 _____ old.

12. We _____ interesting topics.

13. Do they _____ notes in class?

14. _____ he work on Thursday?

15. Isabella _____ to this university.

16. She _____ math.

17. I study hard _____ December.

18. The party is _____ the 16th.

C Family Members

1. Write the names of four of your immediate family members and four extended family members below.

Immediate Family	Extended Family
_____	_____
_____	_____
_____	_____
_____	_____

2. Your partner is at your house for a dinner party. The family members above are also there. Tell your partner who each person at the party is (their name, age, job/major, and any other information).

3. Now change roles. Ask questions about your partner's family members.

D What We Do

1. Write down two things you do every week and when you do them. Tell a classmate.

   In / On _____, I _____.

   In / On _____, I _____.

2. Write down two things your classmate tells you.

   In / On _____, she / he _____.

   In / On _____, she / he _____.

3. Now find a partner. Ask your partner about his or her classmate's weekly activities. Answer questions about your classmate's weekly activities.

E My Imaginary Family

Pretend the people below are your family. Write four sentences to explain their appearance, age, year in school, or birthday.

The man with short black hair is my brother Eric.
He is 33 years old.

1. _____

2. _____

3. _____

4. _____

MODULE 3 AROUND CAMPUS

Module 3 Goals

Understand and use numbers in times
Understand simple words and phrases like *excuse me*, *sorry*, and *thank you*
Use short, memorized phrases for specific purposes with reasonable accuracy
Indicate time by such phrases as *three o'clock*
Build a basic vocabulary of words and phrases about personal details and simple everyday situations
Very simply describe where you go to school
Write about yourself and where you go to school using short, simple phrases
Ask and answer simple questions on very familiar topics (for example, student life) with help

Preview

Look at pages 64 to 89. What pages are these things on?

four clocks _____

a long bridge _____

phrases used on the phone _____

things outside on a college campus _____

Discuss

Talk about the questions with a partner.

1. Where do you think the people are?
   I think the … are …

2. What subject do you study most?
   I study … most.

3. What else is in the building where you have class?
   In the …, there is/are …

4. Who do you talk to on the phone?
   I talk to … on the phone.

5. Where do you go to spend time outside?
   I go to … to spend time outside.

   _____

Unit 5

Unit 6

Scan the QR code to watch a preview video.

★ Unit 5 · Doing Things at School ★

Lesson 1 — Telling Time

A — Model Conversation

Read the conversation. Then listen. 🎧 Track 47

Sophia: Hey Miguel, what time is it?

Miguel: It's quarter past three.

Sophia: Then I should go. My English class starts at 3:30.

Miguel: My math class starts then, too. So what time do you finish today?

Sophia: Around seven o'clock.

Miguel: Wow, that's a really long day!

Sophia: Yeah. I need some coffee, but I don't have time right now. Maybe after this next class.

Miguel: Then I'll meet you at quarter to five at the café.

> **Brief note**
> "Around" means not exactly. It means a little before or a little after.

B — Vocabulary

Listen to the conversation again. Then fill in the blanks with vocabulary words or phrases.
🎧 Track 47

3:15 p.m.
quarter past three

3:30 p.m.
half past three

4:45 p.m.
quarter to five

7:00 p.m.
seven o'clock

math

English

1. It's _____ now.

2. Sophia and Miguel's classes start at _____.

3. Miguel's class is _____.

4. Sophia's class is _____.

5. They are meeting at _____ at _____.

6. Sophia's classes finish at _____ today.

> **Brief note**
> Times before noon end in a.m.; times after noon end in p.m.

C — In Your World

Fill in the blanks. Then practice saying the times by discussing the questions with a partner.

1. What time is it now?   It's _____.

2. _____ when you finish class?   It's _____.

Grammar

what time questions and their answers

what time questions	answers
What time is it?	It's **6:15**.
What time does your class finish?	It finishes **at half past one**.
What time do you start class?	I start **at quarter to nine**.
What time do you want to meet?	Let's meet at **quarter after six**.

> **Brief note**
>
> You can also say times using only numbers. For example, 6:15 is "six-fifteen."

E **Grammar Practice**

Put the words in order to complete the question/answer pairs. Then listen and check.

🔘 Track 48

1. Q: What time do you wake up?   A: at / I / up / wake / past / seven / quarter

   _____.

2. Q: class / time / does / what / your / start / history   A: It starts at 11:30 a.m.

   _____?

3. Q: eat / what / do / time / you / lunch   A: I usually eat at noon.

   _____?

4. Q: What time do you finish for the day?   A: half / usually / past / I / three / at / finish

   _____.

F **Use the Language**

Talking about when things happen

Discuss the pictures below using the given words and (English) language you know.

sunrise

wake up

shower

sunset

dinner

club/party

A Model Conversation

Read the conversation. Then listen. 🎧 Track 49

Anna: So, what other classes do you have?

Travis: I take biology, history, computer science, and economics. You?

Anna: Chemistry, French, philosophy, and math. So I guess we only have English together.

Travis: Seems so. Well, anyway, what do you usually do after class?

Anna: I usually just go home. I take the bus. But on Tuesdays I go to work first. What do you do?

Travis: On Tuesdays and Thursdays I play soccer after class. Maybe we can study on Mondays after class sometimes.

Anna: Sounds like a great idea.

B Comprehension

Listen to the conversation again. Write the name of the student (Anna or Travis) next to the subject they take, or write *both*. 🎧 Track 49

Subject	Student	Subject	Student	Subject	Student
philosophy		history		biology	
economics		math		French	
chemistry		computer science		English	

C Vocabulary: University subjects

Study the words. Listen and repeat. Then try to add more subjects. 🎧 Track 50

geometry

physics

music

geography

art

biology

literature

astronomy

Other subjects

_____

_____

_____

_____

D About You

Answer each question with a sentence. Then talk about your day with a partner.

1. What do you do before this class? _____

_____

2. What do you do after this class? _____

_____

Grammar

Simple present: *go* and *do*; *before* and *after* phrases

Some words with similar spellings have different sounds. For example, the *-o* in *go* and the *-o* in *do* sound different.

The things you usually do and the order you do them in are your *routine*.

subject	verb and information	*before* or *after*
I	**go** to work	**before** class.
You	**do** your homework	**after** dinner.
He/She	**goes** to a café	**after** class.
It	**does** get busy	**before** 8:00 a.m.
We	**do** the laundry	**after** exercising.
They	**go** to the library	**before** lunch.

Grammar Practice

Circle the correct answers.

1. We (do / go) to the library after class.

2. What (do / go) you do on Thursdays after work?

3. Where (do / go) you (do / go) after English class?

4. I exercise early in the morning, (before / after) class.

5. He (does / goes) to work (before / after) class two nights a week.

6. I brush my teeth (before / after) breakfast, just (before / after) leaving home.

7. What bus (do / go) you take in the morning? Do you take the same one (before / after) school?

Use the Language

Your class schedule

Write the names and times of some of your classes.

Class	Days	Start	End
_____	_____	_____	_____
_____	_____	_____	_____
_____	_____	_____	_____
_____	_____	_____	_____

One-letter abbreviations for days:
M – *Monday*
T – *Tuesday*
W – *Wednesday*
R – *Thursday*
F – *Friday*
M-W means *from Monday to Wednesday*, etc.

Now choose a partner. Tell your partner about your classes. Write down your partner's classes.

Class	Days	Start	End
_____	_____	_____	_____
_____	_____	_____	_____
_____	_____	_____	_____
_____	_____	_____	_____

A Model Conversation

Read the conversation. Then listen. Track 51

Emma: Where do you study after class, Stefan?

Stefan: I always study here at the library in the evenings.

Emma: Yeah, I see you come in sometimes when I leave. I'm usually here in the afternoon. I hardly ever find a desk, though.

Stefan: It's usually pretty busy in the afternoon.

Emma: Yeah. So sometimes I go home early and study there.

Stefan: Going home early is nice. I try to go home by nine o'clock, but occasionally I don't go until around ten.

Emma: Wow! That's a long day.

Stefan: Yeah. I'm always tired. But I never let it slow me down!

B Vocabulary

Read. Then write the adverb of frequency next to the percentage of time it represents.

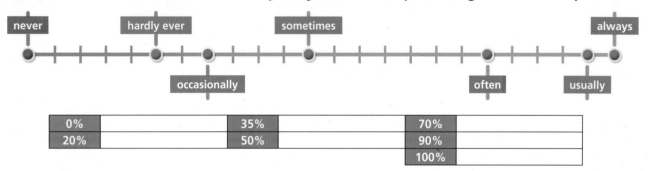

0%		35%		70%	
20%		50%		90%	
				100%	

C Comprehension

Listen to the conversation again. Then fill in the blanks using vocabulary from above. Track 51

1. Stefan _____ studies at the library.

2. Emma _____ visits the library in the afternoon.

3. She _____ gets a desk.

4. Emma _____ studies at home.

5. Stefan _____ goes home at ten o'clock.

6. He _____ lets tiredness slow him down!

D About You

Write down one thing you never do, one thing you always do, and one thing you sometimes do. Then share with a partner.

I never _____.

I sometimes _____.

I always _____.

E Grammar

how often and adverbs of frequency

Brief note

With adverbs of frequency, placement can be flexible. See the Grammar Reference (p. 122) for more information on how to use them with verbs that are not *be*. For *be* verbs, see Unit 6 Lesson 3.

How often questions are often, but not always, answered with adverbs of frequency.	
How often do you go to the movie theater?	We go to the movie theater **often**.
How often do you study in the library?	I **usually** study there.
How often does your study group meet?	On Mondays and Thursdays. / Twice a week.
other words for *usually*	other words for *hardly ever*
a lot	seldom
frequently	rarely

F Grammar Practice

Put the words in order to make sentences.

1. we / to / often / café / after / go / class / the _____.

2. movie theater / sometimes / I / go / the / to _____.

3. often / work / do / go / how / you / to _____?

4. study / past / I / midnight / seldom _____.

5. how / you / break / do / your / together / often / take _____?

6. frequently / home / get / I / late / Fridays / on _____.

G Use the Language

How often do you…?

Consider the following questions, and then fill in the table below.

- What are some things that you do?
- Where do you go?
- How often?

Adverb	Activities
always	
usually	
often	
sometimes	
occasionally	
hardly ever	
never	

Now discuss your activities with a partner.

A   Model Conversation

Read the conversation. Then listen. 🔘 Track 52

Man: See that building? The science labs and classrooms are in there.

Woman: Oh, right. Just where the map says it is. How many floors is it?

Man: The lab tower has five floors, and the classroom tower has three.

Woman: Do you know if there are restrooms nearby?

Man: Yes, they're in the lobby near the elevators.

Woman: Oh. Well, my class is in the second-floor classroom wing.

Man: Just so you know, each floor has a men's room and a women's room across from the elevators.

Woman: That's great to know. Are there stairs too?

Man: Yes, the stairwell is down the hall from the elevators. There are signs on the door.

B   Vocabulary

Study the words. Listen and repeat. Then try to add more vocabulary about buildings.
🔘 Track 53

common area

reception
lobby

stairs
hallway

tower

floors

Other words

_____

_____

_____

_____

_____

C   In Your World

Think of a building on your campus. Write three sentences to describe it. Then your partner asks questions and tries to guess which building your sentences describe. Some examples are below.

Sentences	**Questions**
It's a tall building. There are two elevators.	How many floors does the building have? Does it have a large lobby?

Grammar

More *where* questions and their answers

where questions	answers
Where is the restroom?	It is **across** the hall.
Where are the offices?	They are **on** the third floor.
Where is it?	It's **beside** the library.
Where is that?	It's **inside** the Sciences Building.
prepositions often used to answer *where* questions	

across	beside	on	inside (of)	outside (of)	from
to	down	through	up	at	in

> **Brief note**
>
> Use *at* for a place:
>   *It's at the bus stop.*
> Use *in* for a place with boundaries:
>   *It's in the classroom.*
> Use *on* for surfaces:
>   *It's on the wall.*

> **Brief note**
>
> Look back at pages 15 and 28. This page reviews and adds to information on those pages.

Grammar Practice

Circle the correct prepositions.

1. The science lab is (in / at / on) the building beside the cafeteria.

2. The swimming pool is (in / on / from) the sports center.

3. The clock tower is (in / on / up) the Student Building.

4. The fountain is (inside of / through / on) the courtyard.

5. Are the restrooms (up / down / beside) the information desk?

6. The geography lecture is (in / beside / from) the auditorium.

7. How do we get to the library (down / from / on) the Student Building?

8. The theater is (across / through / inside of) the Performing Arts Building.

Use the Language

Library tour

Work with a group. Imagine you are giving a tour of your school's library to new students. Think about the following questions:

- How many floors does the library have?
- Where are the elevators and the stairs?
- Where are the restrooms?
- Where are the classrooms?
- Where are the study rooms?
- Where is the loan desk?

Tell them where things are in the building. Then switch roles.

A Model Conversation

Read the conversation. Then listen. 🔘 Track 54

Woman: Excuse me. Can you help me find the Psychology Building?

Man: Sure. This is the Humanities Building. Go back out the main doors, and walk past the fountain to the sidewalk. Turn left and follow the sidewalk until you see a large, brick building on your right. That's the Psychology Building.

Woman: Thanks. That sounds easy. Do you know what floor the main lecture hall is on?

Man: Sure. It's on the second floor. Go through the main doors, and at the end of the hall, take the stairwell up. The lecture hall is just in front of the stairwell door.

Woman: Thanks very much!

B Vocabulary

Study the words, phrases, and expressions. Then fill in the blanks below.

Verbs							
go	get	take	turn	walk (past)	pass	find	follow

Phrases		
Excuse me. / Pardon me. I can't find... / Can you help me find...? How do I find...? / How do I get to...? Do you know where...?	How can I help you? How may I help you? First... Then... Next... Then / Next, take the...	to the left to the right on the left on the right

Prepositions and prepositional phrases				
back	behind	at the top of / at the bottom of / at the end of	until	in front of

Man: Excuse me. ❶ _____ the basketball court?

Woman: It's ❷ _____ this building, so ❸ _____ through the main lobby ❹ _____ you get to the back doors. ❺ _____ turn ❻ _____. ❼ _____ the tennis courts. The basketball court is ❽ _____.

Man: Okay. Thanks!

Now listen and check. 🔘 Track 55

C In Your World

Choose a place below. Tell your partner how to get to that place from your classroom.

the restrooms

the stairs

the exit

the elevator

D Grammar

More *how* questions and their answers

Brief note

Put the verb first when giving directions, advice, or commands. The subject is assumed to be *you*.

using *how* to ask for directions	using imperatives to give directions
How do you get there?	**Go** down the hallway.
How do I find the cafeteria?	**Take** the stairs up to the next floor.
How do I reach the loan desk?	**Walk** past the elevator.
How do we find the library?	**Head** to the Science Building. It's on your left.
How do I get to the women's restroom?	**Go** halfway down the hall. **Look** on your right.

E Grammar Practice

Put the words in order to make sentences.

1. elevator / take / down / the / floor / first / to _____.

2. the / how / I / to / bookstore / get / do _____?

3. down / walk / hallway / the / turn / and / right _____.

4. sidewalk / the / past / follow / fountain / the _____.

5. find / I / Student / how / do / the / Building _____?

F Use the Language

Your campus

In groups of three, draw a map of your campus. Discuss where each building is, and then label the buildings. Put a red dot on the building where your classroom is.

Choose a building—not the building you are in now. Write directions about how to get there from here.

_____

_____

_____

_____

Listen to the conversation. Fill in the missing words. Then practice the conversation with a partner. (Track 56)

Man: Excuse me. Hi, I'm a new student here. _____ _____ _____ _____ the Science Building?

Woman: Actually, I'm a science student, so I know the building well. It's that tall tower over there. It has ten _____. Just _____ past the library and _____ _____ a right. _____ _____ the _____ and walk _____ the fountain, and you're there.

Man: Great. Do you know where the _____ _____ is?

Woman: It's _____ the security _____ in the _____.

Man: Okay. I also have to meet someone in the common area there. _____ _____ _____ _____ _____ the common area?

Woman: It's on the _____ _____. Take the _____ up. Then walk down the _____, past the _____ room. The common area is _____ _____ _____, next to the _____.

Man: Awesome! Thanks for your help!

Woman: You're welcome. Have a nice day.

Now write down some places on your school campus that you know how to get to. Imagine you are a new student, and ask your partner how to get to those places. Your partner can check online for a campus map and use it to give you directions. Are the directions good?

Switch roles and practice again.

Some Module 3 Goals in Unit 5

Put a check mark (✓) next to the things you can do.

_____	Understand and use numbers in times
_____	Indicate time by such phrases as *three o'clock*
_____	Build a basic vocabulary of words and phrases about personal details and simple everyday situations

A Read to Write

Read the paragraph about Martin Stein.

My Friend Martin's Routine

My friend Martin has an interesting job. He is a television news reporter. He usually wakes up early and goes to the broadcast studio by 8:00 a.m. Then he reads and watches the news or makes phone calls to get ideas for stories. After he gets an idea, he often goes out to meet and interview people. Then he goes back to the studio to write and edit the story. It airs on the news at 6:00 p.m. Martin watches the story and takes notes. He wants the next story to be better. Martin usually doesn't go home before 8:00 p.m. He works a lot, but he enjoys his job.

B Prewrite

Make notes about the routines of people in your life.

A family member Name: _____	
A friend Name: _____	
A classmate Name: _____	
A famous person Name: _____	

Brief note

Use your imagination for this last one. ☺

C Now Write

Choose one of the people above. Write a short paragraph about that person's routine. Write everything you can write in three minutes. Then stop.

Title : _____

_____

_____

_____

_____

_____

Whose paragraph sounds the most correct? Does your teacher agree?

Lesson 1 The computer lab smells new.

A Model Conversation

Read the conversation. Then listen. Track 57

Stephanie: Hey, Yakov.

Yakov: Oh, hey Steph. How are you?

Stephanie: Not great. I have to write a paper tonight. Actually, I need a place where I can type. Is there a computer lab in this building?

Yakov: Yeah, there's one on the fifth floor. It's at the end of the hallway, near the professors' offices and the study rooms.

Stephanie: Oh, right. I think I know that lab. It looks big.

Yakov: It is. It's also quiet—great for writing! And it's new. It even smells new because the computers are new. They're fast, too.

Stephanie: It sounds nice. Is it crowded?

Yakov: Sometimes, but it's empty at night.

B Vocabulary

Study the words and phrases. Listen and repeat. Then try to add more things that are in your building. Track 58

| water fountain | study room | office | computer lab | floor |

Other things

_____
_____
_____

C Common Adjectives

Listen to the conversation again. Fill in the blanks with adjectives from the top row. Then write the opposites from the bottom row. Track 57

quiet	clean	big	long	new	fast	empty
dirty	small	loud	slow	crowded	short	old

1. The computer lab looks _____.
2. The lab is _____—great for writing!
3. And it's _____.
4. So the computers are _____.
5. At night, the lab is _____.

opposites

1. _____
2. _____
3. _____
4. _____
5. _____

D In Your World

Choose a room in this building or another building you know. Write three adjectives to describe it. Choose a partner and talk about your room. Then change roles.

The _____ is _____, _____, and _____.

Grammar

Adjectives and linking verbs

be + adjective		
subject	*be* verb	adjective
The library Our classroom	is	quiet. small.
The elevators in this building The computers in the lab	are	slow. fast.

linking verb + adjective		
Linking verbs are not action verbs. They are used with adjectives to describe things.		
subject	linking verb	adjective
The study rooms This test These French fries My bed The computer lab The other classroom	look seems taste feels smells sounds	clean. difficult. good. / delicious! warm. new. loud.

Brief note

When we talk about food, *good* is normal. *Delicious* means very good.

Grammar Practice

Put the words in order to make sentences.

1. students / those / are / loud

   _____.

2. pizza / my / tastes / great

   _____.

3. lab / the / is / computer / empty

   _____.

4. classroom / hot / this / feels

   _____.

Now use the noun and adjective to make your own sentences.

5. house / big

   _____.

6. elevator / slow

   _____.

Use the Language

Describing rooms

Write simple descriptions of the pictures. Then choose a partner and talk about your descriptions.

_____ _____ _____

_____ _____ _____

_____ _____ _____

_____ _____ _____

Lesson 2 — Could I speak to Dr. Roberts?

A   Model Conversation

Read the conversation. Then listen. 🔊 Track 59

Lisa: Good morning. This is Lisa in the English Department. How can I help you?

Jesse: Hi. My name is Jesse Robles. I'm in one of Dr. Roberts' classes. May I speak to him, please?

Lisa: I don't think he's here right now. Can I take a message?

Jesse: Yes, I have a question for him about the assignment due tonight. Can he call me back?

Lisa: Sure. Could I have your phone number, please?

Jesse: Yes, it's 555-383-6701.

Lisa: 555-383-6701?

Jesse: That's right.

B   Vocabulary: On the phone

> **Brief note**
> When you know the person you're talking to, say "This is…" When you don't know the person, say "My name is…"

Study the expressions. Then listen and practice. 🔊 Track 60

Answering	Asking for a message
Good morning. This is Lisa. / Hello. Lisa speaking.	Can I take a message?
Calling	**Asking for a phone number**
Hi. My name is Jesse Robles. / Hello. This is Jesse Robles.	Could I have your phone number, please?
Asking to speak to someone	**Giving your phone number**
May I speak to him, please? / Is he in? / Is he there?	My (phone) number is 555-383-6701.
Saying someone is busy	**Saying goodbye**
I don't think he's here right now. / Sorry, he isn't available.	Thank you. Have a good day. / Thanks. Talk to you later.

C   Pronunciation

Phone numbers

Read. Then listen to the phone numbers below and practice. 🔊 Track 61

Numbers for counting are spoken like this:
   103 → *one hundred (and) three*

Phone numbers are spoken using just the numbers:
   103 → *one zero three* or *one oh three.*

Sometimes people say pairs of numbers like real numbers. We usually don't do this for pairs of numbers that have a zero:
   6701 → *sixty-seven oh one*   9943 → *ninety-nine forty-three*   5002 → *five zero zero two*
                                                                             NOT *fifty zero two*

1. 215-686-8021   **2.** 717-503-9843   **3.** 013-8857-6478

D   In Your World

With a partner, write a short phone conversation on a separate piece of paper. Include a simple question, like *What time does class start*? Also include a greeting and a farewell. Then role-play the conversation. Try to do it without reading.

E Grammar

Adjectives before nouns

<table>
<tr><th colspan="3">forming phrases</th></tr>
<tr><th>article/demonstrative</th><th>adjective</th><th>noun</th></tr>
<tr><td>a
that
a
(none)</td><td>polite
big
quick
crowded</td><td>woman
building
question
classrooms</td></tr>
<tr><th colspan="3">in statements</th></tr>
<tr><td colspan="3">The teacher is a polite woman.
Our classroom is in that big building.
I have a quick question.
Crowded classrooms are usually loud.</td></tr>
</table>

Other adjectives

_____

_____

_____

_____

_____

_____

_____

F Grammar Practice

Use the words in the box with _is_ and _a_ or _an_ to make statements.

chair comfortable she friendly Dr. Roberts this busy professor woman

1. _____ .

2. _____ .

3. _____ .

G Listen to Speak

Listen to a description of Dr. Roberts' office. Write the missing adjectives. 🔊 Track 62

Dr. Roberts' office is nice. He has ❶ _____ bookshelves along the wall. There are two ❷ _____ chairs for students to sit in. He also has a lot of ❸ _____ pictures on the wall. There is a ❹ _____ lamp on his desk, and a window behind his chair. It helps make the room bright. On the other wall, there is a table with ❺ _____ books and magazines on it. The only sound is the fish tank in the corner. Otherwise, it's a very ❻ _____ room.

Describe the office in three sentences to your partner.

_____

_____

_____

_____

A Vocabulary: Things in a student lounge

Read. Then listen and repeat. Track 63

pool table

bulletin board

coffee maker

vending machines

coffee table

lounge chairs

TV

sofa/couch

B Listening

Listen. Match the locations with the vocabulary words. Track 64

1. in my building   •   • **a.** pool table
2. at the front of the room   •   • **b.** bulletin board
3. in front of the chairs   •   • **c.** vending machines
4. in the kitchen area   •   • **d.** coffee maker
5. in the corner   •   • **e.** coffee table
6. hanging on the wall   •   • **f.** sofa
7. in the back of the room   •   • **g.** TV
8. along the back wall   •   • **h.** student lounge

Brief note

Bulletin board is another word for announcement board (see p. 26).

C Pronunciation

Compound noun stress

Listen and put a check mark next to the stress you hear. Track 65

1. ☐ LOUNGE chairs   ☐ lounge CHAIRS   4. ☐ vending maCHINES   ☐ VENding machines
2. ☐ COFFee table   ☐ coffee TAble   5. ☐ bulletin BOARD   ☐ BULLetin board
3. ☐ coffee MAker   ☐ COFFee maker   6. ☐ POOL table   ☐ pool TAble

D In Your World

Look back at part A. Which things are in your building? Write two, and add one more thing not from the lesson.

┌─────────────┐ ┌─────────────┐ ┌─────────────┐
│   │ │   │ │   │
└─────────────┘ └─────────────┘ └─────────────┘

Grammar

Adverbs of frequency with *be*

Adverbs of frequency usually come right after *be*.

subject	*be* verb	adverb of frequency	more information
There	is	always	food in the vending machines.
There	are	usually	people in the lounge.
I	am	often	in class.
Our tests	are	sometimes	difficult.
The lab	is	rarely/seldom	crowded.
We	are	never	late.

The words *usually* and *sometimes* can also appear at the beginning of a sentence.

usually or *sometimes*	subject	*be* verb	more information
Usually	there	are	people in the lounge.
Sometimes	our tests	are	difficult.

> **Brief note**
>
> Adverbs of frequency can come in different places. You can learn more later in the *Blueprint* series!

Grammar Practice

Underline the error in each sentence. Write the correct sentence on the line below.

1. Always there are people in the lab.

   _____

2. The lounge never is crowded.

   _____

3. There are events on weekends never.

   _____

4. Seldom I am at the library.

   _____

5. Our tests are easy usually.

   _____

6. There is someone usually on the sofa.

   _____

Use the Language

Describing places

What do you do on the weekend? Think of a place where you spend time. Take notes in the top box, and use them to describe the place to a partner. Then listen to your partner's description and take notes.

> **I am usually at...**
>
> _____

> **My partner is usually at...**
>
> _____

A   Model Conversation

Read the conversation. Then listen. 🔊 Track 66

Student: Excuse me.

Woman: Hi, how can I help you?

Student: Is there a shuttle bus to go to the train station?

Woman: Yes, there's one outside. It stops in front of the student center—right at the front door.

Student: Oh, I see. How often does it come?

Woman: Here's the schedule. Let's see… The next one is at 4:30.

Student: How much does it cost?

Woman: It's free with a student ID.

Student: Oh, okay. Great. Thanks!

Brief note

"Free" means you don't pay money for it.

B   Vocabulary

What else is usually in a student center? Think of some things and add them to the list.

front door / front entrance

Things in a student center

- information desk   - bus schedule
- _____
- _____
- _____
- _____

Then listen to the words your teacher says. How many did you think of?

C   Common *How* Questions

Match the beginnings and endings to make *how* questions. Then fill in the blanks to complete the answers.

1. **Q:** How many •   • **a.** is it to the city?
2. **Q:** How much •   • **b.** does it take?
3. **Q:** How old •   • **c.** does it cost?
4. **Q:** How often •   • **d.** siblings do you have?
5. **Q:** How far •   • **e.** does the bus come?
6. **Q:** How long •   • **f.** are you?

A: _____ _____ three siblings.
A: It _____ $7.00.
A: _____ _____ 21 years _____.
A: It _____ every thirty minutes.
A: It's thirty kilometers from here.
A: It _____ ten minutes.

D   About You

Complete the *how* questions. Then ask and answer them with your partner.

How far is it from your house to…?   It's… from my house to…

How much does it cost to…?   It costs… to…

Grammar

More *how* questions: *how* + adjective/adverb

with *do*				
	adj/adv	*do/does*	subject	verb
How	often	do	you	study?
	often	does	the bus	come?
	long		it	take to get to the city?
	much			cost to get a taxi?

with *be*			
	adj/adv	*be* verb	more information
How	far	is	it to the city?
	crowded		the lounge?
	often	are	you late?
	old		you?
	many		there?

Quick Review

Look at the *how* questions in the two grammar tables. Which *how* question is covered in...

Unit 3 Lesson 1? How _____...?

Unit 4 Lesson 1? How _____...?

Unit 5 Lesson 3? How _____...?

Grammar Practice

Fill in the blanks to form *how* questions.

1. How much _____ it cost?

2. How far _____ _____ to the train station?

3. _____ big _____ your university?

4. _____ often _____ we take tests?

5. _____ _____ does it take to get to the campus?

6. _____ _____ siblings _____ you have?

Use the Language

Asking for information

Choose a place nearby for your partner to go to. Write it on a piece of paper. Give the paper to your partner.

When you receive your paper, ask your partner questions to find out where the place is and how to get there.

Write some of your conversation below.

A: _____

_____

B: _____

_____

A: _____

_____

B: _____

_____

It's a really nice day.

A Model Conversation

Read the conversation. Then listen. Track 67

Jessica: Hi, Ben.

Ben: Hey, Jessica. What's up?

Jessica: Not much. You?

Ben: Uh, well, exams start next week. I like to study out here on the grass.

Jessica: Great idea. It's a really nice day. It's very sunny, though.

Ben: Oh, I usually sit under a tree so I don't feel hot. Sometimes there are empty benches in the shade.

Jessica: Ah, that sounds nice.

Ben: Do you want to join me?

Jessica: Well, I should be going. I have a really big test, too. But I usually study in my dorm.

Ben: Okay. Well, have a good day. Enjoy the weather.

Jessica: You too! Talk to you later.

> **Brief note**
>
> "What's up?" is a casual greeting similar to "How are you?" A common answer is, "Not much."

B Vocabulary

Study the words and phrases. Then listen and repeat. Track 68

courtyard

dorm/ residence

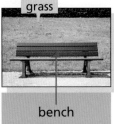
flowers/ flower bed

grass

bench

tree

shade

sidewalk/ walking path

Which of the things above can be found on your university campus? Where are they?

C Vocabulary: Weather

Listen and practice saying the weather phrases. Track 69

 It's sunny.
The sun is out/shining.

 There's a storm.
It's stormy.

 It's windy.

 It's cloudy.

 It's foggy.

 It's hot.
It's warm.

 It's rainy.
It's raining.

 It's snowy.
It's snowing.

 It's cold.
It's cool.

D Quick Review

Look back at the brief notes in this unit. Find words or phrases that mean...

...food is really good: _____   ...announcement board: _____

...something doesn't cost anything: _____   ..."How are you?": _____

Grammar

Intensifiers

We use intensifiers to make words stronger. We can put them before adjectives and adverbs.

really/very/so + adjective		
subject + *be* verb	intensifier	adjective
It's	**really**	sunny.
	very	hot.
	so	windy.

Very and *really* can also be used between an article and an adjective before a noun.

really/very + adjective + noun				
subject + *be* verb	article	intensifier	adjective	noun
He's	a	**very**	smart	professor.
It's		**really**	nice	day.

F **Grammar Practice**

Put the words in order to make sentences.

1. person / very / a / kind / Marie / is

   _____.

2. are / these / nice / flowers / so

   _____.

3. is / hot / classroom / really / our

   _____.

4. very / my / old / dorm / is

   _____.

Rewrite the sentences with intensifiers to make them stronger and more descriptive.

5. The campus is big.

   _____.

6. The trees on campus are tall.

   _____.

G **Listen to Write**

Listen to a woman describing her favorite place to spend time outdoors. Which place is she describing? Track 70

Think of an outdoor place where you like to spend time. Write a description. Then tell a partner.

_____

_____

_____

A College Brochure

Read the university brochure and answer the questions below.

Academic Buildings

<u>**The Science Center**</u>

- New chemistry & biology labs
- Media center
- Computer science lab

<u>**The Humanities Building**</u>

- Philosophy Department
- History library

<u>**The Language Building**</u>

- Classrooms with media/technology
- Library of foreign literature
- International lounge

Sunnybrook University

<u>**Student Center**</u>

- Gym (open 24 hrs.)
- Meeting rooms for student clubs
- Cafeteria & coffee shop
- School supplies store
- Auditorium
- Shuttle bus to city of Sunnybrook

Residence Halls

<u>**Sunnybrook Hall**</u>

- Men's & women's dorms
- Lounge & study rooms

<u>**The West Residence**</u>

- Women only
- TV/movie lounge

<u>**The East Residence**</u>

- Men's & women's dorms
- Lounge with game room & kitchen

Beautiful Campus
with open, green space

1. Which building has a computer lab?
   _____

2. Which building has a place to exercise?
   _____

3. Which residence doesn't have rooms for men?
   _____

4. Which residence has places to do schoolwork?
   _____

B Write a Brochure

Work with a partner. Make a similar brochure for your university.

C Reminder

Some Module 3 Goals in Unit 6

Put a check mark (✓) next to the things you can do.

_____ Very simply describe where you go to school

_____ Ask and answer simple questions on very familiar topics (for example, student life) with help

_____ Use short, memorized phrases for specific purposes with reasonable accuracy

Warm Up

In part B, a student describes his favorite place to study. Put a check mark next to the words you think he's going to use. Then write two more words.

- [ ] quiet
- [ ] hot
- [ ] coffee maker

- [ ] comfortable
- [ ] desk
- [ ] window

- [ ] TV
- [ ] clean
- [ ] sofa

- [ ] _____
- [ ] _____

B Listen for Information

Listen to a student describe his favorite place to study. Make a list of the things the student mentions and the adjectives he uses. Track 71

nouns	adjectives
_____	_____
_____	_____
_____	_____
_____	_____
_____	_____

Listen once more and make sure your list is complete. Check your guesses from part A. Are they correct? Which picture does the student describe? Track 71

C Prepare

Think of a place where you like to study. Write some notes about it, and prepare to describe it.

_____

_____

_____

_____

D Speak

Share your description with a partner.

A Vocabulary

Remember and write...

1. ...two ways to say 3:30 p.m.

   _____ _____

2. ...five school subjects.

   _____ _____ _____ _____ _____

3. ...five adverbs of frequency.

   _____ _____ _____ _____ _____

4. ...five common adjectives.

   _____ _____ _____ _____ _____

5. ...two things that are in a university building. Then flip through the module and write three more.

   _____ _____ _____ _____ _____

6. ...two things that are outside on a university campus. Then flip through the module and write three more.

   _____ _____ _____ _____ _____

B Grammar

Look back at the module. Fill in the blanks.

1. What _____ do you start class?

2. Let's meet at _____ after six.

3. My class is _____ / _____ lunch.

4. He _____ to work two days a week.

5. I usually _____ home after class.

6. Where _____ you go before class?

7. The restroom is _____ the hall.

8. Take the _____ to the fifth floor.

9. The computers in the lab _____ fast.

10. These French fries _____ good.

11. May I _____ to him, please?

12. Could I _____ your number please?

13. My _____ is 555-383-6701.

14. Our tests _____ sometimes difficult.

15. Usually _____ are people in the lounge.

16. How _____ does it cost?

17. How _____ does it take?

18. It's _____ windy today.

C Schedule Interview

First, prepare an interview. Look back to Unit 5. Find questions about habits and routines (for example, *What do you do after class?*). Write the questions below, or make your own questions. Then interview a classmate about his or her daily schedule.

	Questions	Partner's Answers
1.	_____	_____
2.	_____	_____
3.	_____	_____
4.	_____	_____

D Phone Role-Play

Role-play a phone conversation using the instructions below. Change roles once. Refer back to Lesson 2 of Unit 6 for help.

Student A (caller)

Ask to speak to Tom.
Ask for Tom to call you back.
Give your number.

Student B

Answer the phone.
Say that Tom isn't here. Ask for a message.
Ask for the caller's phone number.
Say thanks and goodbye.

E Describe the Pictures

Write five sentences about the pictures below.

1. _____

2. _____

3. _____

4. _____

5. _____

Module 4 Goals

Understand and use numbers in prices
Buy things in shops where pointing and gestures can support what is said
Ask and answer questions about things shops have
Ask people for things and give them things
Very simply describe where you live
Join simple phrases with words like *and*
Describe what you like and don't like
Describe what you can and can't do

Preview

Look at pages 92 to 117. What pages are these things on?

tigers playing   _____

two kinds of sports   _____

a *No Parking* sign   _____

a house with a red door   _____

Discuss

Talk about the questions with a partner.

1. Look out your classroom window. What are you seeing?
   I'm seeing …

2. What do you want, and where can you get it?
   I want …
   I can get it …

3. What do you have at home?
   I have … at …

4. What food do you like? What food don't you like?
   I like … but I …

5. What can you do well?
   I … well.

   _____

Unit 7

Unit 8

Scan the QR code to watch a preview video.

Lesson 1 Are you going to the cafeteria?

A Model Conversation

Read the conversation. Then listen. Track 72

Samantha: Hey, Ethan! Are you coming to the cafeteria?

Ethan: Oh, hi Samantha. No, I'm not. I'm just going into the library. Where are you heading?

Samantha: I'm meeting Kelly and Philip for lunch.

Ethan: It's 3 o'clock. Are you having a meal together?

Samantha: No, just a snack. Anyway, come with us.

Ethan: Sorry. I want a book for my African literature class.

Samantha: Oh, are you studying African literature?

Ethan: Yeah. I'm taking Professor Dayo's class. We're discussing Western African writers this month.

Samantha: That's great. Well, they're waiting for me. I should be going.

Ethan: All right. See you later.

> **Brief note**
> "Heading" is informal. It means going.

B Vocabulary

Listen to the conversation again. Then fill in the blanks with vocabulary words or phrases. Track 72

cafeteria

snacks

alone / by himself

literature

meal

together

writer

Ethan and Samantha are discussing their plans. Samantha is heading to the **a** _____. She's meeting her friends Kelly and Philip there. They're having a **b** _____ together, not a **c** _____. Ethan is going to the library **d** _____. He's **e** _____ a book for his African **f** _____ class.

looking for

C About You

With a partner, answer the questions about what you're doing right now and nowadays.

- How are you feeling?
- Is your English improving?
- Are you studying any other languages?
- Are you reading anything interesting lately?
- Are you living by yourself nowadays?

> **Brief note**
> *Right now* means at this exact time; *nowadays* means in the recent past and the near future.

Grammar

Present continuous tense

questions	answers	statements
Be + subject + *-ing*...?	*Yes/No*, subject + *be* (*not*) (+ *-ing*...)	Subject + *be* + *-ing*...
Am I **dancing** well?	Yes, you **are** (**dancing** well).	You**'re dancing** very well.
Are you **going** home now?	No, I**'m not** (**going** home).	I**'m not going** home right now.
Is Jessica **studying** history this semester?	Yes, she **is** (**studying** history).	She**'s studying** history.
Are the children **sleeping**?	No, they**'re not** (**sleeping**).	They**'re not sleeping.** They're **playing.**

E **Grammar Practice**

Use *be* and the *-ing* forms of the verbs to make questions and answers.

1. **read**

    Q: _____ you _____ a book?   A: No, I _____.

2. **run**

    Q: _____ the dog _____?   A: Yes, it _____ in the park.

3. **speak**

    Q: _____ speaking too loudly?   A: No, you _____ speaking too loudly.

4. **play**

    Q: _____ those two _____ a game? A: Yes, _____ chess.

F **Use the Language**

What are they doing?

1. With a partner, look at the pictures below and say what the people and animals are doing.

Group A

Stella | Andrew and Lev | a couple | Beth | Mr. and Mrs. Scott | tigers

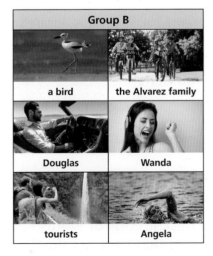

Group B

a bird | the Alvarez family | Douglas | Wanda | tourists | Angela

2. Student A, close your book. Student B, quiz your partner about all of the Group A pictures. Ask yes/no questions about what the people are doing. Can your partner remember? Examples: "Is Stella eating soup?" "Are the tourists taking pictures on a beach?"

3. Switch roles. Student B, close your book. Student A, look at your book and quiz your partner about the Group B pictures.

In the Library

A Model Conversation

Read the conversation. Then listen. 🔊 Track 73

Ethan: Excuse me. Can you help me find a book?

Librarian: Maybe. Which one are you looking for?

Ethan: I'm preparing for my African literature class, so I'm doing some research. I'd like a book called *Things Fall Apart*, but I don't remember the author's name.

Librarian: It's Chinua Achebe. I'm just going to check the computer... Oh, we don't have it right now. I'm sorry.

Ethan: Oh, no. Well, can I reserve the book? I'd like it by Wednesday. I want it before the first day of classes.

Librarian: I can put you on the waiting list. Until then, would you like a study guide for the book?

B Vocabulary

Study the words and phrases. Fill in the blanks below. Then listen. 🔊 Track 74

Things in the library			
librarian	shelf (shelves)	library card	waiting list
Book information			
title	subject	author	call number
Actions			
check out / borrow	return	look for	reserve
Statuses		**Dates**	
due	on loan	due date	check-out date

1. There are many books on this library's _____.

2. When you want help, the _____ can help you.

> **Brief note**
> Remember (see p. 43), the plural of *shelf* is *shelves*.

3. The book you want is _____ right now. The _____ is September 28th.

4. The _____ of my favorite book is *War and Peace*, and the _____ is Leo Tolstoy.

5. At our library, a book is _____ exactly twenty-one days after the _____.

C Vocabulary Comprehension

Listen to the descriptions of words related to the library. For each question below, choose the word that best fits the description: 🔊 Track 75

1. a. subject   b. library card
   c. due date   d. shelf

2. a. author   b. subject
   c. call number d. title

3. a. waiting list b. subject
   c. due date   d. call number

4. a. reserve   b. look for
   c. borrow   d. return

D Grammar

Brief note

We use *would like* when we want something, but we don't use *wouldn't like* when we don't want something.

want and *would like*

affirmative			negative		
I / You / We / They	**want**	ice cream.	I / You / We / They	**don't want**	these shoes.
He / She / It	**wants**	a toy.	He / She / It	**doesn't want**	sugar.
I / You / We / They / He / She / It	**would like**	some coffee.	(See the brief note above.)		
The short form of *would* is often used: *I'd like ice cream. / We'd like some coffee.*					

questions and answers						
Do	I / you / we / they	**want**	ice cream?	**Does**	he / she / it	**want**	some coffee?
Yes, ____ **do**. / No, ____ **don't**.				Yes, ____ **does**. / No, ____ **doesn't**.		
Would	I / you / we / they / he / she / it			**like**		some coffee?
Yes, ____ **would**. / No, ____ **wouldn't**.						

E Grammar Practice

Fill in the blanks using a pronoun, *want*, or *would like*. For some questions, more than one answer is possible.

1. Isabelle and Esther are hungry. _____ some spaghetti.

2. Peter is *not* thirsty. _____ any water.

3. I _____ a book about Columbus. I need it for my history class.

4. They _____ coats because it is very hot today.

Fill in the blanks to make questions and answers.

5. Q: _____ Nancy and Owen want chicken?   A: Yes, they _____.

6. Q: _____ want new shoes?   A: No, I _____.

7. Q: _____ she like an umbrella?   A: Yes, I'm sure she _____.

8. Q: Do we all _____ soup with dinner?   A: No, _____. David _____ a salad.

F Use the Language

In another place

Now imagine that you and your partner are at the beach, the supermarket, or the bookstore. Practice asking your partner what he or she wants or would like. Then report your partner's answers to the class.

Lesson 3   At the Cafeteria

A   Model Conversation

Read the conversation. Then listen. ⊙ Track 76

Samantha: Hi, Kelly. Where's Philip?

Kelly: He's studying for an important test.

Samantha: Oh. Well, I'm hungry. What are they serving today?

Kelly: Let's see… It looks like salad or sandwiches here. There are noodles, stir-fried meat, and some kind of soup over there.

Samantha: What kind of soup is it?

Kelly: It's green. I don't know. Pea soup, maybe.

Samantha: Oh, I don't like that. What about the stir-fry? What kind of meat is in it?

Kelly: The sign just says "meat." I don't know what kind.

Samantha: I want to know what kind of food I'm eating. Let's try the Chinese restaurant across campus.

B   Vocabulary

Study the words. Then listen and repeat. ⊙ Track 77

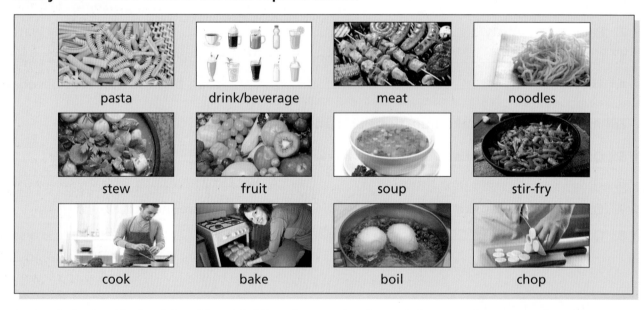

pasta	drink/beverage	meat	noodles
stew	fruit	soup	stir-fry
cook	bake	boil	chop

Now circle the kinds of food (or drink) and put a check mark next to the ways of cooking. (Hint: stew and stir-fry are both foods and ways of cooking.)

C   About You

Discuss food, cooking, and eating with a partner.

Conversation starters:

- What kinds of food do you eat a lot?
- What kinds of food can you cook?
- What kinds of restaurants do you like?
- Write another question about food: _____?
  Ask your partner the question.

> **Brief note**
>
> In questions, use *kind* and a singular noun when you want only one answer; use *kinds* and a plural noun when you want two or more answers. (The noun *food* is uncountable. See Unit 7 Lesson 5 to learn more about uncountable nouns.)

D Grammar

Questions with *what* and *what kind (of)*

What...?			
Questions with *what* can have general answers (A: *What is it?* B: *It's a piece of fruit.*) or specific answers (A: *What is it?* B: *It's an apple.*). Sometimes the answer doesn't give enough information.			
What kind of...?			
What kind of asks for a description or for more information. The answer can be a description, or it can be a *kind* or *type* of thing. For example, there are many *kinds* of fruit. Apples are one *kind*.			
example questions and answers			
A: **What** do you want to eat?	B: I want soup.	A: **What kind of** soup do you want?	B: I want chicken soup.
C: **What** is that?	D: It's an animal.	C: **What kind of** animal is it?	D: It's a squirrel.
E: **What** are you reading?	F: A magazine.	E: **What kind of** magazine?	F: A fashion magazine.

E Grammar Practice

Fill in the blanks to make questions and answers.

1. Q: _____ job do you want?

    A: I _____ a safe, easy _____.

2. Q: _____ would you like?

    A: I _____ something to drink.

3. Q: What _____ are you reading?

    A: I _____ a mystery novel.

4. Q: _____ place does he live in?

    A: _____ a small apartment.

5. Q: _____ are they shopping for?

    A: _____ for meat and vegetables.

6. Q: _____ dog do you want?

    A: I don't want a dog. I want a cat.

F Use the Language

Questions with *What kind of...?*

Choose one of the questions below and ask your partner general questions. Then use *what kind of* questions to get more information. Take notes on your partner's answers.

- Classes
- TV and movies
- Things you spend money on
- Things you want
- What you do every day

Notes:

Using your notes, write a paragraph about your partner.

_____

_____

_____

_____

_____

Lesson 4   At the Restaurant

A   Model Conversation

Read the conversation. Then listen. 🔊 Track 78

Host: Welcome to Hunan Delight. We have a lunch buffet until 2:00 p.m. Would you like that, or do you want something from our lunch menu?

Samantha: I don't know. Kelly, which would you like?

Kelly: I think I'd like something from the menu.

Host: Okay. There are a few tables open. Which table would you prefer?

Kelly: One near a window.

Host: How's this one?

Samantha: Perfect.

Host: Great. Your waiter is just getting you some water. Oh, another customer is coming in. I should be going.

Samantha: Thank you. Wow, Kelly. There are so many things on the menu. Do you know what kind of food you want?

Kelly: I think I want seafood.

Samantha: Which seafood dish?

Kelly: Maybe the grilled fish.

B   Vocabulary

Study the words and phrases. Then listen and repeat. 🔊 Track 79

Actions		Kinds of food		Things in the restaurant		
serve	order	seafood	dessert	buffet	host	menu
greet	select	salad	meat dish	server (OR waiter [man], waitress [woman])		item

C   Vocabulary Comprehension

Fill in the blanks with words from above.

1. Give food to guests: _____

2. Decide what you want: _____

3. A list of food or drinks: _____

4. This person serves customers in a restaurant: _____

5. Fish is a kind of _____.

6. You can use many vegetables in a(n) _____.

7. Steak is a kind of _____.

8. One thing on a list or menu: _____

9. Many items on a table; customers put items onto a plate and carry it to their table: _____

10. Meet customers and welcome them: _____.

D   In Your World

How does it taste? With a partner, arrange the food items according to their taste. Then discuss what kinds of food you prefer.

Sweet	Sour	Spicy	Salty

Food items			
popcorn	vinegar	curry	potato chips
ice cream	cola	candy	chili peppers
pretzels	lemon	lime	hot sauce

98

Grammar

Questions with *what* and *which*

Brief note

Limit is used to reduce the answer you will get. For example, the question *What do you want?* has many answers; *Which shirt do you want?* asks for a specific of shirt.

What...?	*Which...?*
does not limit the answer	limits the answer to certain choices or a category

What do you want?
    I want candy.
 What do you read in your free time?
    I read my email.
 What do you usually watch?
    I watch sports.
	Which shirt do you want?
	    I want the red shirt.
	 Which book are you reading?
	    I'm reading *Huckleberry Finn*.
	 Which TV show do you want to watch?
	    I want to watch *Saturday Night Live*.

Grammar Practice

Look at the answers. Use the words in the box to make questions.

country	visiting	does	want	which	what	are
serves	which	restaurant	seafood	you	he	

1. Q: _____ ?   A: I'm visiting Portugal.

2. Q: _____ ?   A: Some pizza.

3. Q: _____ ?   A: The Seven Seas Buffet.

Use the Language

Which do you like more?

Look at the pairs of pictures. Write a word for each picture. Then find a partner. For each pair, tell your partner which one you like more. Give reasons.

Sports

Homes

Foods

Fruits

Movies

Clothing items

A Model Conversation

Read the conversation. Then listen. Track 80

Samantha: Hey, Ethan. What are you drinking?

Ethan: I'm having an Americano. Join me. The coffee is really good here.

Samantha: How much is it?

Ethan: Three dollars for an Americano. I don't know what the other stuff costs.

Samantha: I want a shot of espresso. In fact, I think I want more than one.

Ethan: How many are you going to have?

Samantha: Two right now. Maybe more later. I also want some cake. No, I think I want a donut. Oh, I want to go to the bathroom. Can you order for me?

Ethan: Uh, sure. How many donuts?

Samantha: Just one for me. No, two. Sorry. Hey, order one for you, too. I'm paying for it.

B Vocabulary

Study the words and phrases. Then listen and repeat. Track 81

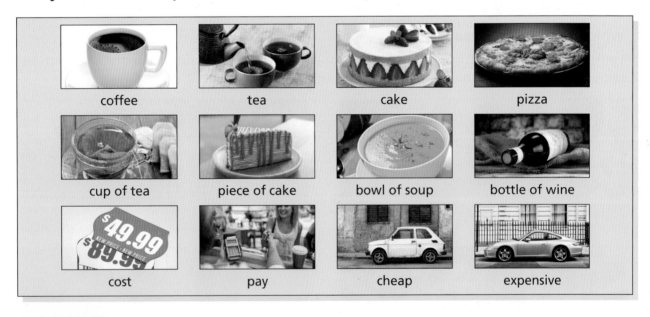

coffee

tea

cake

pizza

cup of tea

piece of cake

bowl of soup

bottle of wine

cost

pay

cheap

expensive

C About You

1. With a partner, make a list of things you sometimes buy and a list of things you want.

I buy...

I want...

2. Which of these things are cheap, and which are expensive? How much do you think they cost?

Grammar

Questions with *how many* and *how much*; uncountable nouns

how many	how much	units
We use *how many* to ask about items that can be counted. *Few* is the opposite of *many*.	We use *how much* to ask about things that cannot be counted. *Little* is the opposite of *much*.	Most uncountable things can be measured using units. To ask about units, we use *how many*.
Examples: birds, fingers, restaurants, children, books **How many** birds...?	Examples: water, time, money, pasta, cake **How much** water...?	Examples: bottles of water, hours, dollars, plates of spaghetti, pieces of cake **How many** bottles of water...?

> **Brief note**
>
> Units generally occur in this structure:
> number or article + unit(s) + *of* + item
>
> Remember, the item is singular but the unit can be plural, depending on the word(s) before it. For example, we say *a cup of coffee* but *three cups of coffee*.

E **Grammar Practice**

For each question, decide which answer choices are correct and which are wrong. (Hint: More than one answer could be correct.) With your teacher, talk about why.

1. How much _____ do you have?
   a. free time   b. library books   c. American money

2. How _____ bottles of water are you buying?
   a. much   b. many   c. little

3. How many _____ does Hector have?
   a. sisters   b. homework   c. cake

F **Use the Language**

How much do you need?

1. Write down four things you want to do.

   _____   _____

   _____   _____

2. Ask and answer questions about how much time, money, or energy you need to do these things.

3. You can answer using "a lot," "a little," "not much," or units.

4. Look at the things you want to do and at the pictures below. To do these things, what do you need besides time, money, and energy?

Listen to a conversation between a waiter and two customers. Fill in the blanks with the words that you hear. Track 82

Waiter:	_____ _____ _____ to order?
Mr. Jones:	Not yet. We're having trouble _____ _____ _____. My wife would like something spicy. I _____ _____ anything spicy, but I would like some seafood.
Waiter:	All right, I'm happy to help. First, we have three items _____ _____ _____ that are spicy. We have many _____ _____ _____. The Arrabbiata spaghetti is very good.
Mrs. Jones:	I'm not in the _____ for pasta. _____ else do you have?
Waiter:	We have a spicy stew, and chicken with chili.
Mrs. Jones:	_____ _____ do they cost?
Waiter:	The chicken with chili costs _____ _____. The stew is nineteen dollars. It's a _____ _____, and it's very spicy. Do you know _____ you would like?
Mrs. Jones:	I think I want the stew.
Waiter:	Very good. And now for the seafood. _____ _____ many kinds. There's the lobster…
Mr. Jones:	Is that expensive?
Waiter:	It's _____ dollars.
Mr. Jones:	What other kinds of seafood do you _____?
Waiter:	We have _____ pasta and—if you look at your menu here—this grilled fish with lemon is very good.
Mr. Jones:	Is it a salty fish?
Waiter:	It's a salty fish, yes.
Mr. Jones:	I like that. _____ _____ _____ the spicy beef stew and the fish with lemon.

Answer the following questions about the conversation above.

1. Why does the waiter help Mr. and Mrs. Jones?
2. What kind of food does Mrs. Jones want?
3. Why doesn't she order the pasta?
4. Which is the most expensive item, and how much does it cost?
5. Which item would you like to order, and why?

Find a partner. On a separate piece of paper, design this restaurant's menu.

- Use all of the items from the conversation, and add some items of your own.
- Include prices for each item.
- When you finish, play the roles of waiter and customer, and try ordering from the menu you designed.

Some Module 4 Goals in Unit 7

Put a check mark (✓) next to the things you can do.

_____ Buy things in shops where pointing and gestures can support what is said

_____ Ask and answer questions about things shops have

_____ Describe what you like and don't like

Prepare

Do you want to be a customer or a clerk? Choose one role. Then find a partner who wants the other role.

Read to Speak

Look at the boxes below. Prepare for your role as a clerk or a customer.

Clerk				
• Choose three books. Your store does not have those books. Put an X through their titles. • Write in a price between $7.50 and $40.00 for each book. • Do not show your final list to your partner.				
Title	**Author**	**Kind of book**	**Price**	**Other information**
War and Peace	Leo Tolstoy	Novel		Russian literature
Things Fall Apart	Chinua Achebe	Novel		African literature
1776	David McCullough	History book		Subject: American history
A Little History of the World	Ernst Gombrich	History book		Subject: World history, Easy to read
In Cold Blood	Truman Capote	True Crime		You want it for an American literature class.
The Autobiography of Malcolm X	Malcolm X with Alex Haley	Biography		Malcolm X was a famous African-American.
Lives of the Artists	Giorgio Vasari	Biography		Subject: Leonardo da Vinci, Michelangelo, and other artists
Steve Jobs	Walter Isaacson	Biography		Steve Jobs started the Apple computer company.

Customer	
• Select three books from the list above. Write their information in the space below. • Select one kind of book you want more information about. • You do not know the price of any books until you ask your partner.	
Book you want:	**What you know about this book:**
1. Title: Author:	You know the title and author.
2. Title:	You know the title only.
3. Author: Other information:	You don't remember the title.
4. Kind of book:	You want to know the titles of books of this kind.

Practice Speaking

Use the information from part B to role-play a conversation between a customer and a clerk in a bookstore. Continue until the customer uses all of his or her information from part B. Then practice again.

Now Speak

Stand up in front of the class with your partner. Role-play your conversation, asking about only two books. After all the pairs finish, discuss these questions:

A. Which pairs are fast? Do they make many mistakes?
B. Which pairs don't make many mistakes? Are they fast?

| Lesson 1 | Going Home |

A Model Conversation

Read the conversation. Then listen. Track 83

Student: Taxi! Thanks for stopping.

Taxi driver: Sure. Where are you going?

Student: To Rose Street. The address is 7147 Rose Street Southwest.

Taxi driver: Is that a house or an apartment?

Student: It's a house. About how much is it going to cost to get there, and how long is it going to take?

Taxi driver: I can't say for sure. It's really going to depend on traffic. So, are you a student?

Student: Yes, I am.

Taxi driver: What are you studying?

Student: I'm studying business and math.

B Vocabulary

Listen to the conversation again. Then fill in the blanks with vocabulary words. Track 83

street

address

house

apartment

Taxi driver: Hi. Where are you going?

Student: I'm going to Rose ❶ _____.

Taxi driver: What's your ❷ _____?

Student: My address is ❸ _____ Southwest.

Taxi driver: Is that a ❹ _____ or an ❺ _____?

What's your address?

_____

_____

Now find a partner. Take turns being the taxi driver and the student. Then try again with your own address.

C Vocabulary: Modes of transportation

Brief note

We can also use the verb *riding* for bicycles, motorcycles, horses, and a few other things.

How are you getting (home, to school, to work, etc.)?

Going now	Going later	
I'm in a taxi, car, etc. I'm driving.	I'm going on foot.	I'm going by bus, subway, taxi, car, etc.
I'm on a bus, the subway, etc.	I'm walking.	I'm taking a bus, subway, taxi, etc.
I'm on foot, my motorcycle, my bike, a horse, etc.	I'm driving.	I'm taking my car, motorcycle, bicycle, etc.

Grammar

Present continuous in information questions, including subject questions

present continuous in information questions		
Information questions are sometimes called *wh-* questions. They ask for details. The answer is never just *yes* or *no*.		
information question	**short answer**	**complete sentence**
What is she **studying**? **Where are** you **going**? **How are** you **doing**? **When are** we **going** home?	Business and math. To Rose Street. Fine. Soon.	She **is studying** business and math. **I'm going** to Rose Street. I **am doing** fine. We **are going** home soon.
information questions: subject questions		
One kind of information question is a subject question. Subject questions ask about the person (or thing) that is doing the action. These questions often start with *who* or *what*.		
subject question	**short answer**	**complete sentence**
Who is studying business?	Cathy. / Cathy is. (Cathy is the **subject**; we know what Cathy is doing from the question.)	Cathy is studying business.

Grammar Practice

Fill in the blanks with words from the box to make questions and answers.

about	going	is	where	who	is
what	thinking	going	what	I'm	reading

1. Q: _____ are you _____? A: _____ to class.

2. Q: _____ is sitting next to you? A: Mike _____. That's his desk.

3. Q: _____ are you _____ about? A: About lunch—I'm hungry!

4. Q: _____ is she _____ right now? A: A new book. She says it's good.

Use the Language

What are they doing?

With a partner, discuss the people's names and what they're doing. Then tell your class. Does everyone have the same story as you?

A Authentic Text: Signs

Read the signs. Discuss their meanings with a partner.

No Smoking

Do Not Enter

Yield

Do Not Litter

No Parking

Stop

B Vocabulary

Study the words and phrases. Then fill in the blanks below.

parking

yield

smoking

litter

trash can   enter

1. There is no _____ on this street from 3 p.m. to 5 p.m.
2. "Do not _____" means do not go into a street or place.
3. It is not nice to _____ the park with trash.
4. There is no _____ in this restaurant.
5. Don't litter. Use a _____.
6. To _____ means to let another person go first.

C Vocabulary in Context

Write words for each sign.

1. _____

2. _____

3. _____

Which signs can you see on your school campus? Where are they?

D   Grammar

Negative imperatives; conjunction *or*

negative imperatives	
Do not / Don't + verb	Don't smoke; Don't drink; Do not litter; Do not enter
No + *-ing*	No smoking; No drinking; No talking; No parking
conjunction *or*	

DRINK OR DRIVE DO NOT DRINK AND DRIVE	The word *or* introduces a choice: *Do you want coffee **or** tea?* (Which one?) *Let's watch TV **or** go to a movie.* (not both) *I want to play basketball, soccer, **or** baseball.* (only one of them, not all three)
	With *No* and *Don't*, *or* joins nouns and verbs: ***No** dogs, cats, **or** other pets. **No** smoking **or** drinking.* ***Don't** talk **or** make noise. **Don't** smoke **or** drink.*

E   Grammar Practice

Fill in the blanks with the correct forms of the verbs.

1. No _____ or _____. (talk, text)

2. Don't just _____ there. _____ something! (stand, do)

3. Do not _____ here! (park)

4. No _____, _____, or _____. (eat, drink, litter)

Now write the correct words.

5. _____ smoking in this room!

6. _____ work too much.

F   Use the Language

Making rules

On a separate piece of paper, write ten rules for your classroom. Share your rules with classmates. Then, with your class, agree on ten rules. Write the final list below.

Rules

1.

2.

3.

4.

5.

6.

7.

8.

9.

10.

A   Model Monologue

Read the monologue. Then listen. 🔊 Track 84

Sylvia: My house is small, but it's warm and comfortable. It has a kitchen, a living room, and two bathrooms. Upstairs there are three bedrooms, but there are only two people living here. The third bedroom is our study. We use it to do homework, watch TV, or just relax. There is no smoking in my house, and no parking next to the front door. We don't litter, and we don't play loud music. We eat downstairs, in the kitchen or in the living room. Sometimes I have a snack in my bedroom. I like my house. Do you like your house?

B   Vocabulary

Study the words and phrases. Then listen and repeat. 🔊 Track 85

kitchen

upstairs

downstairs

living room

bedroom

bathroom

home office / study

C   Vocabulary Comprehension

Where do people do these things? Fill in the blanks below with vocabulary words. There can be more than one correct answer, and sometimes you need prepositions or articles, too.

1. eat _____

2. sleep _____

3. do homework _____

4. brush teeth _____

5. cook _____

6. take a shower _____

D   In Your World

Ask about a partner's house. How many bedrooms are in it? How many bathrooms? Is there a kitchen? A living room? A study? Stairs? Is your partner's bedroom upstairs or downstairs? Are there any other rooms in the house? After you finish, tell your partner about your house.

Grammar

Conjunctions *and* and *but*

and		but	
joins a list of two or more words		**joins opposite phrases and ideas**	
hamburger, fries, **and** Coke work, study, **and** sleep		He was tired, **but** he kept studying. It was cold, **but** we went outside anyway.	
joins related phrases or ideas		**means *except for***	
He's living in America, **and** he's learning English. It's very hot **and** sunny today.		Every student knows the correct answer **but** Mary. I like every class **but** history.	

Grammar Practice

Write *correct* next to the correct sentences. Next to the incorrect ones, write the correct conjunction.

1. _____ He likes soccer, and his son does not.

2. _____ We want to go swimming, but it's raining right now.

3. _____ Carlos but Jorge are coming for dinner.

4. _____ Everyone but Diego is here.

5. _____ They love to travel, but they're going to Africa next month.

6. _____ Get me a sandwich, salad, chips, but a soda.

Use the Language

Find the differences

Work with a partner. Find twelve differences in the sets of pictures. Make a list and share it with your class. Do any groups have anything on their list that you don't have on yours?

Quick Review

Look back at the brief notes in this module.

1. What is an informal way to say "going"? _____

2. List three things we can ride: _____ _____ _____

A Model Monologue

Read the monologue. Then listen. [Track 86]

Andre: When I get home from school, the first thing I like to do is relax. I usually listen to music. Sometimes, after hearing the music, I want to play my guitar. Other times I ride my bike. I like exercise, but I don't like to jog. My roommate and I always have a big dinner. After that, we often play video games. Sometimes we watch TV or a movie. Before going to bed, I usually just read a book or a magazine. I love reading! It's one of my favorite things to do at home.

B Vocabulary: Hobbies

Study the words and phrases. Then listen and repeat. [Track 87]

relax

play guitar

watch TV

read a magazine

go to the movies

play video games

listen to music

ride a bike

jog

hang out with friends

Brief note

Bike is a short, easy way to say *bicycle*.

C Comprehension

Look back at part A. Follow the instructions below. Then answer the questions.

1. In the vocabulary section, put a check mark next to the pictures of things Andre likes to do.
2. Put an *X* next to the pictures of things Andre doesn't like to do.
3. Put a question mark (*?*) next to the things Andre doesn't discuss.
4. Do you have a check mark, an *X*, or a question mark next to *go to the movies*? (yes / no) Explain.
5. Do you have a check mark, an *X*, or a question mark next to *hang out with friends*? (yes / no) Explain.
6. Andre discusses hobbies that are not in the vocabulary section. What are they?

D Vocabulary in Context: Charades

Play in groups. Take turns acting out a hobby while other students try to guess what your hobby is. The first student who guesses correctly takes the next turn.

Example answers: *You are watching TV.*   *You're riding a bike.*   *You are jogging.*

Grammar

Simple present: *like* in statements and questions

like / don't like + noun	*like / don't like* + to + verb
I **like** books. She **likes** the Chinese guy. I **don't like** jogging. He **doesn't like** movies.	I **like** to read. **Does** Amanda **like** to go shopping? **Do** you **like** to play video games? **Does** Roberto **like** watching television?

When we really like something, we often say we love it:
    I like reading, but I love watching movies!
When we really don't like something, we often say we hate it:
    I like reading magazines, but I hate reading books!	

F **Grammar Practice**

Put the words in order to make sentences or questions. In the last blank, write your answer to the question.

1. and / writing / like / reading / I

   _____.

2. to / doesn't / Pablo / sing / like   singing / he / hates

   _____. _____.

3. English / do / like / you / book / your

   _____?

   Your answer:

   _____.

G **Use the Language**

What are your hobbies?

1. List five hobbies below, on the left side. Use two from part B, and write three other hobbies that you know.

2. Talk to a partner or in a group. Do people in your group like the hobbies on your list? Take notes about their answers below, on the right side.

3. When you're finished, report your results to the class.

Five hobbies		Notes
1.		
2.		
3.		
4.		
5.		

A Model Monologue

Read the monologue. Then listen. 🔊 Track 88

James: When we make dinner at my house, we all help. Every person has a different job. I can cook vegetables, but I can't cook meat. I usually burn it. One of my roommates, Jongwon, is Korean. He can cook great meat! He usually barbecues it. My other roommate, Henry, can't cook meals, but he makes great desserts. We have big dinners—we can eat a lot! After dinner, we do the dishes and clean the kitchen. We have a rule in our house: no whining! And after we finish all that work, we're tired. We usually go to the living room and watch TV for a while.

Brief note

"A while" means *a short time*. But not too short—for a really short time, use *a few seconds* or *a few minutes*.

B Vocabulary

Listen to the monologue again. Then match a vocabulary word on the left with a word or phrase on the right. 🔊 Track 88

grill

barbecue

burn

Brief note

Barbecue can be a noun or a verb. As a noun, it can be a kind of party, the meat you cook, or the thing you cook the meat on. As a verb, it can mean to have a barbecue party or to cook food in a barbecue style.
Grill can also be a noun (see the picture) or a verb meaning *to cook on a grill*.

dishes

do/wash the dishes

clean

1. laundry • • a. dirty clothes

2. whine • • b. do

3. barbecue • • c. grill

4. wash • • d. cook too much

5. burn • • e. complain

laundry

do/wash the laundry

whine/complain

Brief note

Remember, *do* doesn't always mean *wash*. But in these phrases, the two words have the same meaning.

C In Your World

With a partner, discuss the questions below. Then report your partner's answers to the class.

Which of the things in the vocabulary section can you do?
Which of those things do you do?
How often?

Notes

Simple present: *can*

can	can't
Can means *able* to do something.	*Can't* means *not able to* do something.
I **can** speak English. She **can** run fast. Birds **can** fly.	I **can't** speak Chinese. He **can't** run fast. People **can't** fly.
In questions: *Can* + subject + verb + ...?	
Can you swim? **Can** Theresa cook? **Can** he write well?	

Brief note

Questions beginning with *can't* are a little different from questions beginning with *can*. You can learn about these questions later in the *Blueprint* series!

Fill in the blanks with *can* or *can't*.

1. I'm usually late to work in the morning. I just _____ wake up on time.

2. I love this spaghetti, Mom. You _____ really cook!

3. He _____ play the guitar very well. In fact, it sounds awful!

4. Birds _____ fly, but many birds _____ also swim.

5. Felicia is a good student. She _____ speak English, and she _____ write it, too.

Read the paragraph. Highlight the words you don't know. Discuss their meanings with your teacher or look them up in a dictionary.

Sometimes I like to eat breakfast food for dinner. I really like omelets, so I can cook them really well. Do you know that you can cook an omelet on a grill? First, turn the heat to medium. Then grill your meat. I like bacon. I cook it on the grill, and then I put a special pan—a skillet—onto the grill. I put butter on it, but you can use oil. After mixing milk, eggs, and pepper (you can add salt, too) in a bowl, pour it into the pan. Move the pan while the eggs cook. You can see when the omelet finishes cooking—it looks wet but the liquid can't move. Then I put the bacon on one side. I add cheese, fold the egg, and then add more cheese. You can sprinkle vegetables on it, too. Then enjoy!

A how-to paragraph

What can you cook? Write a short paragraph about how to cook it.

_____

_____

_____

A A House for Sale

Read the advertisement for a house. Then answer the questions.

> **FOR SALE:** A two-bedroom house. It has two bathrooms, a kitchen, a living room, and a study. It is small but very clean. It is near schools and parks. The address is 312 Northwest 8th Street. Phone Mr. Lopez at 555-2468.

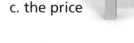

1. Which information is NOT included in the ad?
   a. the number of bedrooms   b. the address   c. the price

2. Which is true about this house?
   a. It is very large.   b. It has a study.   c. It is far from schools.

3. What should a buyer do first?
   a. phone Mr. Lopez   b. pay money   c. drive to the house

B Write an Ad

Pretend you are selling your home, or that your parents are selling their home. Write an advertisement in the space below. Share your ad with a classmate. Discuss the differences.

FOR SALE: _____

_____

_____

_____

_____

_____

_____

C Reminder

Some Module 4 Goals in Unit 8

Put a check mark (✓) next to the things you can do.

> _____ Very simply describe where you live
>
> _____ Join simple phrases with words like *and*
>
> _____ Describe what you can and can't do

Warm Up

What comes next? Write *noun* or *verb*.

can _____   like _____   like to _____

Listen for Information

Listen to the description of Donna. Then fill in the blanks. 🔘 Track 89

1. She _____ to play guitar.

2. She _____ run fast.

3. She _____ to watch TV.

4. She likes to read, and to _____.

5. She _____ cook.

6. She _____ to eat.

Interview Classmates

Interview four classmates. Ask one about three things he or she can do. Ask another about three things he or she can't do. Then ask two others about what they like and don't like.

My classmate

_____

can:

1. _____
2. _____
3. _____

My classmate

_____

can't:

1. _____
2. _____
3. _____

My classmate

_____

likes:

1. _____
2. _____
3. _____

My classmate

_____

doesn't like:

1. _____
2. _____
3. _____

Describe

Tell the class about one of your classmates, but don't say your classmate's name. The class will try to guess who it is.

Module 4 Review

A Vocabulary

Remember and write...

1. ...four messages written on signs.

   _____ _____ _____ _____

2. ...two library book statuses and two actions involving library books.

   _____ _____ _____ _____

3. ...four ways of cooking food.

   _____ _____ _____ _____

4. ...three ways of getting home.

   _____ _____ _____

5. ...four rooms in a house.

   _____ _____ _____ _____

6. ...two types of houses and two hobbies people do in their houses.

   _____ _____ _____ _____

B Grammar

Look back at the module. Fill in the blanks.

1. She _____ a book.

2. _____ the boys _____ a game?

3. I _____ want these shoes.

4. _____ you want to watch TV?

5. Would _____ a cup of coffee?

6. _____ of food do you want to eat?

7. _____ shirt do you like, blue or red?

8. How _____ money do you have?

9. How _____ kinds of food can you name?

10. How are you _____ home?

11. I'm _____ by taxi.

12. I'm _____ a bus.

13. Would you like coffee _____ tea?

14. He likes reading _____ writing.

15. Everyone _____ Helen is coming.

16. No, she _____ like cake.

17. She _____ speak English, and she _____ write it, too.

18. He _____ read, but he _____ write.

116

C Chain Game: *I can...*

Play in groups or as a class. The first person says, "I can _____." The second person repeats and adds a new verb: "I can (first person's word) and _____." The third player says, "I can (first person's word) and (second person's word) and _____," etc. Play until you can't remember your classmates' verbs. Then try again.

D Shopping Role-Plays

Choose six food and drink items from Unit 7. Choose a price for each item. Work in pairs. Do **not** show your items and prices to your partner. Take turns "shopping."

Do you have...?   *Yes, I do / No, I don't...*

How much...?   *It costs...*

                           The price is...

Now work in a group of three. Take turns being a waiter and customers in a restaurant. Use words from Unit 7.

Do you want...?   *Would you like...?*   *I want... I'd like...*

Which kind...?

E About a Menu

Write two sentences and a question about the items on the menu.

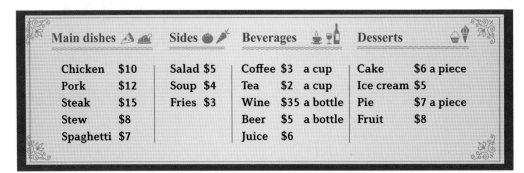

Main dishes		Sides		Beverages			Desserts	
Chicken	$10	Salad	$5	Coffee	$3	a cup	Cake	$6 a piece
Pork	$12	Soup	$4	Tea	$2	a cup	Ice cream	$5
Steak	$15	Fries	$3	Wine	$35	a bottle	Pie	$7 a piece
Stew	$8			Beer	$5	a bottle	Fruit	$8
Spaghetti	$7			Juice	$6			

1. _____

2. _____

3. _____

Unit 1

New People

Lesson 1 Simple present: *be*

We often use the verb *be* to connect a subject with an adjective or noun that gives more information about the subject.

To form a statement with *be*, use Subject + *am / are / is...*

To form a question with *be*, use *Am / Are / Is* + subject...?

I am a student. → Are you a student?

be questions	answers to *be* questions	*be* statements
Am I a new student?	✓ Yes, you **are** (a new student).	You**'re** a new student.
Are you a chemistry teacher?	✗ No, **I'm not** (a chemistry teacher).	I**'m not** a chemistry teacher.
Is she a woman?	✓ Yeah (, she**'s** a woman).	She**'s** a woman.
Are we classmates?	✗ Nope (, we**'re not** classmates).	We**'re not** classmates.
Are you boys?	✓ Yep (, we**'re** boys).	We**'re** boys.
Are they good friends?	✗ No, they **aren't** (good friends).	They **aren't** good friends.

Lesson 2 Short forms (contractions)

We often use short forms (also called "contractions") in everyday speaking and writing.

We put an apostrophe in place of a missing letter.

I'm a teacher. 　　　　　 *We're classmates.*

subject pronouns	*be* verbs	short forms
I	am	I**'m**
you	are	you**'re**
he / she / it	is	he**'s** / she**'s** / it**'s**
we	are	we**'re**
you (guys/all)	are	you**'re**
they	are	they**'re**

Lesson 3 Short forms (contractions) in negative statements

Sometimes we use *not* with or in contractions.

I'm not a teacher. 　　　　　 *We aren't friends.*

subject pronoun	*be* verb	short form
I	am **not**	I'm **not**
you	are **not**	you**'re not** / you **aren't**
he / she / it	is **not**	he**'s** / she**'s** / it**'s not**
		he / she / it **isn't**
we	are **not**	we**'re not** / we **aren't**
you (guys/all)	are **not**	you**'re not** / you **aren't**
they	are **not**	they**'re not** / they **aren't**

Lesson 4 *be* questions with question words

- *How:* asks about the way in which something happens or for news about someone or something
- *Where:* asks about places
- *What:* asks about things, animals, and actions

Use the question word + *be* + subject to ask *how, where,* and *what* questions about the subject.

Where are you from? 　　　 *How are you?*

What is his job?

question word + *be* + subject + ...	subject + *be* + ...
How are you today?	I'm very well, thanks.
Where is she from?	She's from Colombia.
What is your last name?	It's Ramirez.
Where are we?	We're in the hall.
How are you guys?	We're okay.
Where in Peru **are** they from?	They're from Lima.

Lesson 5 Possessives

Possessives show who or what something or someone belongs to—who owns or has something. We use the possessive case to express possession.

To form a possessive noun, add -*'s* (if the noun is singular) or just -*'* (if the noun is plural).

See you in tomorrow's class. That is my friends' house.

subject pronoun	object pronoun	possessive adjective
I	me	my
you	you	your
he	him	his
she	her	her
we	us	our
they	them	their

singular	plural
my	our
your	your
his / Jameson's	
her / Miss Khalifa's	their / my friends'
its / tomorrow's	

Unit 2
The Classroom

Lesson 1 Articles *a* and *an*

We use the articles *a* and *an* when talking about something for the first time. *A* and *an* mean "one."

Articles come before the noun.

Do you have a pencil? → *Yes, I have a pencil.*

Do you have an eraser? → *No, I don't have an eraser.*

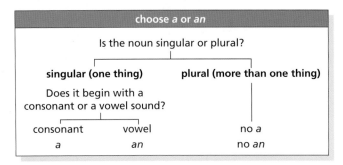

choose *a* or *an*

Is the noun singular or plural?

singular (one thing)   plural (more than one thing)

Does it begin with a consonant or a vowel sound?

consonant   vowel   no *a*
a   *an*   no *an*

Note English vowels are *a*, *e*, *i*, *o*, and *u*, but for articles, the sound is more important than the letter. For example, the word *university* begins with a vowel (*u*), but it sounds like "*yuniversity*," so we use *a*, not *an*.

Lesson 2 Simple present: *have*

We use the verb *have* in a question when asking about possession (things you own or carry).

Do you have a phone?

Does she have a dog?

have questions and answers		*have* statements
Do I / you / we / they **have** a laptop?	✓ Yes, I **do**. (Yep, Yeah) ✗ No, I **don't**. (Nope)	I **have** a laptop. I **don't have** a laptop.
Does he / she / it **have** a bicycle?	✓ Yeah, he **does**. ✗ Nope.	He **has** a bicycle. He **doesn't have** a bicycle.

Note Remember to use an article with a singular noun and *-s* with a plural one.

Lesson 3 Possessives: pronouns and questions

We use possessive pronouns and possessive nouns to ask or talk about ownership.

To ask about ownership, use *whose* + noun + *be* + *it/they*?

Whose books are they? → *Mine. / His. / Jane's.*

questions				possessives	
Whose	noun	*is/are*	pronoun	Mine. Yours. Hers.	Ours. Yours. [*plural*] Theirs.
Whose	backpack	is	it?		
	tablets	are	they?	His. The teacher's.	The students'. Mike and Lisa's.

Lesson 4 Questions and statements with *there is* and *there are*

We use *there is* and *there are* to make statements about a thing.

To form a statement, use *There is/are* + *a/an* + noun.

There is an umbrella.   *There are umbrellas.*

To form a question, use *Is/Are there* + *a/an* + noun?

Is there a student in the hall?

→ *Yes, there is a student in the hall.*

singular noun	**Is there** an elevator?	**There is** an elevator.
plural noun	**Are there** computers?	**There are** computers.

There is has a contraction—*there's*. You can use the contraction *there're* to mean *there are* in spoken English, but don't use it in written English.

Lesson 5 Prepositions of location and prepositional phrases

We use prepositions of location to say where things are. A prepositional phrase often comes after the verb *be*.

My backpack is under the desk.

prepositions of location

Prepositions of location tell where things are. They often come after the verb *be* and before a noun.

My <u>backpack</u> <u>is</u> <u>under</u> the <u>chair</u>.
　subject　*be*　prep.　　noun

A preposition + noun is called a *prepositional phrase*. Prepositional phrases tell where the subject is. With no noun after the preposition, you don't know where the subject is.

My smartphone is in a _____.

Where is the smartphone? Do you know?

Between the preposition and the noun, you often see an article or a possessive adjective.

　　on **a** wall　　　in **my** backpack

Two nouns come after the preposition *between*.

<u>Melissa</u> sits between <u>Juan</u> and <u>Tammy</u>.
　n.　　　　　　　　n.　and　n.

The book is between the pens. (Plural *-s* means more than one pen.)

Unit 3
About Family

Lesson 1 *how many* questions and their answers

We use *how many* when asking about things we can count.

How many + object + *do* + subject + verb...?

How many siblings do you have? → *I have three siblings.*

How many + noun + *is/are there?*

How many donuts are there? → *There are three donuts.*

how many questions	answers to *how many* questions
How many sisters do you have? **How many** pets do you have?	I have **one** sister. I **don't** have **any** pets.
How many cousins do Mark and Natalie have?	They have **four** cousins.
How many people are there in your family?	There are **twenty** people in my family.

Lesson 2 *some* and *any*

We use *some* or *any* when we don't know the number of something. *Some* is often used in positive sentences. *Any* is used in negative sentences and questions.

To form a question with *any,* use *do/does* + subject + have + *any*...?

Does he have any evening classes?

To form a sentence with *some,* use Subject + *has/have* + some + object.

Yes, he has some evening classes.

questions with *any*	answers	statements with *some* and *any*
Do you have **any** classes with Dr. Johnson?	✓ Yes, I do. ✗ No, I don't.	✓ I have **some** classes after lunch. ✗ I don't have **any** classes today.
Does he have **any** relatives here?	✓ Yes, he does. ✗ No, he doesn't.	✓ He has **some** relatives here. ✗ He doesn't have **any** relatives here.

Lesson 3 Questions with *who*

We use *who* to ask questions about people.

To form a question with *who,* use *who* + *is/are* + extra information...?

Who is the man in this video? → *He is our teacher.*

subject	question	answer
singular	Who is **the person** in this picture? Who is **this** next to the chair? Who is **that**?	This / That — is my mom.
plural	Who are **they**? ~~Who are those?~~	These / Those / They — are my parents.

Lesson 4 Plurals

Plurals show when there is more than one thing. We change the ending of a noun to make it plural.

To make a word plural, we usually add *-s, -es, -ies* or *-ves.*

I have one cousin. → *She has three cousins.*

But there are some irregular plurals.

plural spellings		irregular plurals	
+s		child	**children**
group	group**s**		
parent	parent**s**	person	**people**
-x, -s, -ch, -sh → +es			
lunch	lunch**es**	man	**men**
class	class**es**		
-y → +ies		woman	**women**
eighty	eight**ies**		
party	part**ies**		
-fe → +ves			
life	li**ves**		
yourself	yoursel**ves**		

Lesson 5 Describing appearance using *with* prepositional phrases

We use *with* in a prepositional phrase to give details about a person or thing.

Questions with this kind of prepositional phrase have the form *Who* + *is/are* + subject + *with* + object of preposition...?

Who is the woman with the long hair?

Statements with this kind of prepositional phrase have the form subject + *with* + object of preposition + verb + more information.

describing appearance using *with*	
statement + *who* question	*who* question using *with*
A young man has an earring. Who is the man? →	Who is the young man **with the earring**?
A woman has dark skin. Who is the woman? →	Who is the woman **with dark skin**?
two statements	one statement using *with*
A man has no hair. He's my best friend. →	The man **with no hair** is my best friend.
A woman has tattoos. She's my younger sister. →	The woman **with tattoos** is my younger sister.
simple description	description using *with*
that man, the one who has short red hair →	the man **with short red hair**
there is	*there are*
There is a man **with a beard**. →	There are women **with long hair**.

Unit 4
School Life

Lesson 1 Questions with *when* and *how old*

When questions ask about time. *How old* questions ask about age.

It's common to use *be* with these questions.

When is the test?   *How old is the doctor?*

questions with *when* and *how old* + *be*			
question word(s)	*be* verb	subject	answer
When	is	your lecture? the party?	It's on the 23rd. It's on October 14th.
How old	are is	you? your mom?	I'm 21. She's 48 years old.

Note To say a date, use ordinal numbers.

My birthday is July 2nd [second].

To say an age, use a normal (cardinal) number.

She is 19 [nineteen] years old.

Lesson 2 Simple present in affirmative statements

Use the simple present for facts and repeated actions.

For all subjects except 3rd person, use the verb's base form.

I study math.   *They meet in this room.*

singular subject			plural subject		
subject	verb	more information	subject	verb	more information
I	take write	notes. reports.	We	discuss	interesting topics.
			You (guys/ all)	read study	well. hard.
You	practice learn	a lot. quickly.	They	take	a test every month.

Lesson 3 Simple present questions and answers

To form a question in the simple present, use *do* + subject + main verb...?

Do you have class?   *Do they work?*

simple present questions			
Do	subject	main verb	more information
Do	I	need	better grades?
	you	have	classes on Wednesday?
	we	have	a test today?
	you [plural]	need	some apples?
	they	take	things to class?
affirmative and negative answers			
Do I...?		Yes, you **do**. / No, you **don't**.	
Do you...?		Yes, I **do**. / No, I **don't**.	
Do we...?		Yes, you **do**. / No, you **don't**.	
Do you [plural]...?		Yes, we **do**. / No, we **don't**.	
Do they...?		Yes, they **do**. / No, they **don't**.	

3rd person singular uses *does* instead of *do*.

3rd person singular			
Does	subject	main verb	more information
Does	she he	exercise come	on weekends? on Thursday?
answers			
Yes, she / he / it **does**.		No, she / he / it **doesn't**.	

Lesson 4 3rd person singular subjects in simple present affirmative

For 3rd person subjects, do not use the base form of the verb.

Most 3rd person verbs are formed by adding *-s*.

She reads.   *He writes.*   *It works.*

3rd person singular	other subjects
My older brother **works**. Alice **goes** to this university. She **studies** math. She **plays** sports here, too. Giovanna **attends** university.	I **have** two older sisters. You **study** a lot. We **go** out on weekends. They **are** freshmen.

Note Spelling changes for 3rd person singular verbs follow the rules for plurals.

study → studies   watch → watches   push → pushes

Lesson 5 Prepositional phrases of time

You can give times using prepositions.

Use *in the* for *morning*, *afternoon*, and *night*.

I study in the afternoon.   *I go home in the evening.*

Use *in (the)* for seasons.

I take classes in winter.   *Brad works in the summer.*

time of day
in
She works **in the morning / afternoon / evening**.
at (see note)
Alejandro goes out **at night**.
day + time of day
on
I have math class **on Monday morning**.
days & dates
on
We always have quizzes **on Monday**.
The party is **on the 16th**.
The test is **on Friday, December 21st**.
months & seasons
in
Classes start **in January**.
Every year, we visit Japan **in the summer**.

Note For *night*, use *at* without *the*. This is a special rule.

I sleep at night.   *She has classes at night.*

Unit 5
Doing Things at School

Lesson 1 *what time* questions and answers

We use *what time* questions to ask about the time.

To form a *what time* question, use *what time + be/do*...?

What time does your lab start?

What time is the movie tonight?

what time questions	answers
What time is it now?	It's **9:30 / half past nine.**
What time does your practice finish?	It finishes **at 8:45 / quarter to nine.**
What time do you start your lesson?	I start **at eight o'clock.**
What time do you want to go out tonight?	Let's go out **at 7:15 / quarter past seven.**

Lesson 2 Simple present: *go* and *do*; *before* and *after* phrases

Prepositions of time tell us when something happens. We usually use prepositions of time (*before* and *after*) after the main phrase.

I go to practice before school.

subject	verb and information	*before* or *after*
I	**go** to the gym	**before** class.
You	**do** your essay	**after** the meeting.
He/She	**goes** to the club	**after** work.
It	**gets** busy	**before** 7:00 a.m.
We	**go** to the library	**after** class.
They	**do** their homework	**before** soccer games.

Lesson 3 *how often* and adverbs of frequency

We use *how often* to ask about frequency.

To form these questions, use *how often + do/does + subject + verb*...?

How often questions are often, but not always, answered with adverbs of frequency.	
How often do you go to the dance club?	We **seldom** go to the dance club.
How often do you study at home?	I **rarely** study at home.
How often does your study group meet?	On Mondays and Thursdays. / Twice a week.
other words for *usually*	other words for *hardly ever*
a lot	seldom
frequently	rarely

Lesson 4 More *where* questions and answers

We use *where is* or *where are* when we want to know the location of a place or thing. We can also use these questions to get directions.

To form a *where* question, use *where + is/are + place/ thing*...?

Where is the student music hall?

Where are the new bicycle stands?

where questions	answers
Where is the cafeteria?	It is **across** from the main office.
Where are the restrooms?	They are **on** each floor.
Where is it?	It's **outside** the Arts Building.
Where is that?	It's **down** the hall.
common prepositions of place	
across beside on inside (of) outside (of) from	
to down through up at in	

Note Use *at* for a place: It's **at** the bus stop.
Use *in* for a place with boundaries: It's **in** the classroom.
Use *on* for surfaces: It's **on** the wall.

Lesson 5 More *how* questions and answers; imperatives

We often use *how* to ask about directions and feelings.

To form a question with *how,* use *how + be/do + subject + verb*...?

We use imperatives to give directions or instructions to someone.

To form an imperative, use the base form of the verb.

using *how* to ask for directions	using imperatives to give directions
How do you get there?	**Catch** the number 5 bus.
How do I find the field?	**Go** straight down this road and take a left.
How do I reach the travel agency?	**Take** the elevator to the third floor.
How do we find the copy center?	**Head** across this street and go inside the double doors.
How do I get to the dressing rooms?	**Go up** the stairs. They're on the right side of the hallway.

Note If you have to give many directions, use transition words such as *then* or *next* to separate them.
Go left at the intersection. Then go straight for fifty meters.

Unit 6
Places on Campus

Lesson 1 Adjectives and linking verbs

We can use adjectives, like *big* or *slow*, after *be* verbs.

Form statements by using *I am, he / she / it is,* or *you / we / they are.*

I am new.   *It is fast.*   *They are quiet.*

be + adjective		
subject	**be verb**	**adjective**
I	am	**new.**
Our classroom	is	**small.**
You / We / They	are	**quiet.**

linking verb + adjective		
Linking verbs are not action verbs. They are used with adjectives to describe things.		
subject	**linking verb**	**adjective**
The practice rooms	look	**small.**
This homework	seems	**easy.**
These vegetables	taste	**fresh. / great!**
This car seat	feels	**comfortable.**
This food	smells	**good.**
The park across the street	sounds	**quiet.**

Lesson 2 Adjectives before nouns

Adjectives can also come before nouns.

Use article/demonstrative + adjective + noun.

I'm the new teacher.   *This is a fast computer.*

forming phrases		
article/demonstrative	**adjective**	**noun**
a	**friendly**	person
that	**small**	house
a	**big**	problem
(none)	**new**	smartphones
in statements		
The American student is a **friendly** person. My roommate and I share that **small** house. I have a **big** problem. **New** smartphones are usually expensive.		

Note There are special rules about articles. For now, use *the* if you already mentioned the noun. The first time you mention it, use *a(n)* for singular nouns and no article for plural nouns.

Lesson 3 Adverbs of frequency with *be*

Adverbs of frequency tell *how often* something is true. They usually come before an action verb, but after a *be* verb.

We always go to class.   *They are always loud.*

subject	*be* verb	adverb of frequency	more information
There	is	always	food in the vending machines.
There	are	usually	people in the lounge.
I	am	often	in class.
Our tests	are	sometimes	difficult.
The lab	is	rarely/seldom	crowded.
We	are	never	late.

Note *Usually* and *sometimes* may begin sentences.
Usually there are people in the lounge.
Sometimes the teacher is late.

Lesson 4 More *how* questions: *how* + adjective/adverb

How questions can ask about the degree of an adverb.

Use *how* + adverb + *do/does* + subject...?

How often do you work?   *How long does it take?*

with *do*				
How	**adv.**	***do/does***	**subject**	**verb and more information**
How	often	do	you	study?
	often	does	the bus	come?
	long		it	take to get to the city?
	much			cost to get a taxi?

How questions can also ask about the degree of an adjective.

Use *how* + adjective + *be* + subject...?

How big is the classroom?

with *be*			
How	**adj.**	***be* verb**	**subject and more information**
How	far	is	it to the city?
	crowded		the lounge?
	often	are	you late?
	old		you?
	difficult		the tests?

Lesson 5 Intensifiers

We use intensifiers to make words stronger. We can put them before adjectives and adverbs.

The elevator is slow. → *The elevator is really slow.*

really/very/so + adjective		
subject + *be* verb	**intensifier**	**adjective**
It's	**really**	rainy.
	very	cold.
	so	stormy.

Note Do not use *so* this way in formal writing.
Very and *really* can be used before nouns.

really/very + adjective + noun				
subject + *be* verb	**article**	**intensifier**	**adjective**	**noun**
He's	a	**very**	smart	professor.
It's		**really**	nice	day.

Unit 7
Study or Eat?

Lesson 1 Present continuous

We use *be* with the *-ing* form of a verb to talk about action that is ongoing. This combination is called the *present continuous*.

To form questions in the present continuous, use *Am / Are / Is* + subject + (verb)*-ing*…?

He is playing basketball. → *Is he playing basketball?*

questions	answers	statements
Be + subject + **-ing…?**	Yes/No, subject + **be** (not) (+ **-ing…**)	Subject + **be** + **-ing…**
Am I **drawing** well?	Yes, you **are** (**drawing** well).	You**'re drawing** very well.
Are you **going** to school now?	No, I **am not** (**going** to school).	I**'m not going** to school now.
Is Jessica **studying** math this semester?	Yes, she **is** (**studying** math).	She**'s studying** math.
Are the boys **running**?	No, they're not (**running**).	They**'re not running**. They**'re walking**.

Lesson 2   *want* and *would like*

We express desires using *want* (with subject-verb agreement) or *would like* (no subject-verb agreement).

We want spaghetti.   *She would like some water.*

Questions use *do/does* + subject + *want*…? or *would* + subject + *like*…?

Does she want ice?   *Would she like ice?*

affirmative		negative	
I / you / we / they he / she / it any subject	**want** **wants** **would like**	**don't want** **doesn't want** X	a toy.
The short form of *would* is often used: *I'd like ice cream.*		*We'd like some coffee.*	
questions			
Do ___ **want**…? (I / you / we / they)	Does ___ **want**…? (he / she / it)		**Would** ___ **like**…? (*any subject*)
answers			
Yes, ___ **do**. No, ___ **don't**.	Yes, ___ **does**. No, ___ **doesn't**.		Yes, ___ **would**. No, ___ **wouldn't**.

Note Use *don't/doesn't want* as the negative. There is no negative form of *would like*.

Lesson 3   Questions with *what* and *what kind (of)*

We use *what* to ask open-ended questions, and we use *what kind* to get more specific.

We use *what kind of* before a noun to make clear what we are asking.

What are you writing?   *What kind of story is it?*

What…?
This is an open-ended question. The answer can be general ("It is a toy") or specific ("It is a ball").

What kind of…?
What kind of asks for a description or for more information. The answer can be a description, or it can be a *kind* or *type* of thing. For example, there are many *kinds* of toys. A ball is one *kind* of toy.

example questions and answers	
A: **What** are you reading?	A: **What kind of** magazine?
B: It's a magazine.	B: It's a fashion magazine.

Lesson 4   Questions with *what* and *which*

We use *which* to ask a question that clearly expresses the kind of answer we want. The answer should be one specific thing.

Which is used before a noun.

What are you looking for? → *I'm looking for a book.*

Which book are you looking for? → *I'm looking for* War and Peace.

What…?	**Which…?**
does not limit the answer	limits the answer to certain choices or a category
What do you want? I want candy. **What** do you read in your free time? I read my email. **What** do you usually watch? I watch sports.	**Which** shirt do you want? I want the red shirt. **Which** book are you reading? I'm reading *Huckleberry Finn.* **Which** TV show do you want to watch? *Saturday Night Live.*

Lesson 5   Questions with *how many* and *how much*; uncountable nouns

We ask about amounts using *how many* and *how much*.

How many is used with countable nouns. *How much* is used with uncountable nouns. Units such as *bottles* can be used with uncountable nouns such as *water* to make them countable.

How many bottles of water do they have?

How many children are in the classroom?

How much time do you need?

how many	how much	units
We use *how many* to ask about items that can be counted. *Few* is the opposite of *many*.	We use *how much* to ask about things that cannot be counted. *Little* is the opposite of *much*.	Uncountable things can be measured using units. To ask about units, we use *how many*.
Examples: dogs, pencils, houses, people, days	Examples: tea, time, money, paper	Examples: cups of tea, hours, dollars, pieces of paper
How many cats…?	**How much** coffee…?	**How many** cups of coffee…?

Unit 8
Away from School

Lesson 1 Present continuous in information questions, including subject questions

We use the present continuous to talk about something that is happening now. We also use it to explain things that will happen soon. Most information questions in the present continuous have this form: *Wh-* word + *be* + subject + *-ing...?*

What are you doing?

Subject questions have this form: *Wh-* word + *be* + *-ing...?*

Who is teaching the class?

present continuous in information questions	
Information questions are sometimes called *wh-* questions. They ask for details. The answer is never just *yes* or *no*.	
What is she **practicing**? **Where are** they **eating**?	She**'s practicing** the drums. They**'re eating** at a Thai restaurant.
How are you **doing** in your physics class? **How are** we **getting** to the party tonight?	I**'m having** a difficult time. We**'re taking** a taxi together.
information questions: subject questions	
One kind of information question is a subject question. Subject questions ask about the person (or thing) that is doing the action. These questions often start with *who* or *what*.	
Who is he **meeting**?	He**'s meeting** his friend Alex.

Lesson 2 Negative imperatives; conjunction *or*

We use negative imperatives to tell someone NOT to do something.

Don't walk on the grass.

negative imperatives	
Do not / Don't + verb	**Do not** talk in the library. **Don't arrive** late for dinner.
No + *-ing*	**No using** smartphones in class **No swimming** in the lake

We use the conjunction *or* to connect two ideas together. *Or* can mean you have a choice.

Do you want to play tennis or go for a hike?

When we use *or* in a negative, it means both ideas are not allowed.

Do not walk or run on the escalator.

conjunction *or*
The word *or* means a choice: • Do you want milk **or** cream? (Which one?) • Let's play a game **or** watch a video. (not both) • I want to learn saxophone, flute, **or** clarinet. (only one of them, not all three)
With *No* and *Don't*, *or* joins nouns and verbs: • **No** exchanges **or** refunds • **No** standing **or** walking on the bus • **Don't** eat **or** drink on the subway.

Lesson 3 Conjunctions *and* and *but*

The words *and* and *but* connect two ideas. *And* joins two similar ideas. *But* joins two ideas that are opposite or different.

I'm having a sandwich and soup for lunch.

She bought a ticket, but she was late for the train.

and	*but*
joins a list of two or more words	**joins opposite phrases and ideas**
text, e-mail, **and** chat run, jog, **and** work out	I was full, **but** I kept eating. It was cold, **but** we went outside anyway.
joins related phrases or ideas	**means *except for***
They're playing in a band **and** preparing for a concert. It's very hot **and** humid today.	Everyone **but** Chris is seeing the play tonight. (Chris isn't seeing the play.)

Lesson 4 Simple present: *like* in statements and questions

We use the verb *like* in the simple present to talk about things we enjoy.

Do you like listening to podcasts? → *Yes, I do.*

like / don't like + noun	*like / don't like* + *to* + verb
I **like** books. She **likes** the Chinese guy.	I **like** to read. **Does** Amanda **like** to go shopping?
I **don't like** jogging.	**Do** you **like** to play video games?
He **doesn't like** movies.	**Does** Roberto **like** watching television?
When we really like something, we often say we **love** it: "I like reading, but I love watching movies!" When we really don't like something, we often say we **hate** it: "I like reading magazines, but I hate reading books!"	

Lesson 5 Simple present: *can* and *can't*

We use *can* + verb to say that someone is able to do something, or that something is possible.

We use *can't* + verb to form the negative.

We can take the 8:30 bus to Stockholm.

Questions with *can* have this form: *Can* + subject + verb...?

Can he dance well?

can	*can't*
Can means *able* to do something.	***Can't*** means *not able* to do something.
I **can** meet you there today. She **can** learn quickly. Cars **can** go on this road.	I **can't** cook well. He **can't** play for long. People **can't** ride this train.
In questions: *Can* + subject + verb + ?	
Can you ski? **Can** Sam speak Italian? **Can** he play baseball?	

Unit 1
New People

Lesson 1
yep
yeah
nope
people
girl
boy
woman
man
student
teacher
classmate
tutor
boss

Lesson 2
Hello. / Hi. / Hey.
Good morning (afternoon).
How's it going?
How are you (doing)?
(Very) Well/Good.
Not bad.
Okay.
All right.
Thanks.
chemistry
oh
aha
highlight
How/What about you?
Me too.
Not me.
Nice/Good to meet you.
Welcome.
I'm… / My name is…

Lesson 3
marital status
husband
wife
married
single
job
doctor
professor
truck driver
police officer
title
Mr.
Ms. / Mrs. / Miss
Dr.
Prof.

Lesson 4
country
nationality
Brazil – Brazilian
Canada – Canadian
Chile – Chilean
China – Chinese
Colombia – Colombian
Costa Rica – Costa Rican
Egypt – Egyptian
Japan – Japanese
Korea – Korean
Mexico – Mexican
Peru – Peruvian
Spain – Spanish
Thailand – Thai
the United States –
American

Lesson 5
anyway
That's all for today.
We'll stop here.
I should go.
I have to be going.
I've got to get going.
See you (later, etc.).
Have a good…
Good night.
Take care.
Bye. / Goodbye.

Unit 2
The Classroom

Lesson 1
zero
one
two
three
four
five
six
seven
eight
nine
ten
eleven
twelve
thirteen
fourteen
fifteen
sixteen
seventeen
eighteen
nineteen
twenty
twenty-one
twenty-two
twenty-three
twenty-four
twenty-five
twenty-six
twenty-seven
twenty-eight
twenty-nine
thirty
forty
fifty
sixty
seventy
eighty
ninety
one hundred
one thousand

Lesson 2
girlfriend
boyfriend
bicycle
car
airplane
bus card
dog
cat
game console
laptop computer
tablet computer
desktop computer

Lesson 3
red
yellow
blue
green
purple
pink
orange
magenta
gray
black
white
brown
take notes
speaker

Lesson 4
ceiling
clock
light
window
blackboard
announcement board
wall
chair
table
floor
corner
back
aisle
monitor
mouse
podium
steps
keyboard
front

Lesson 5
of course
object
on
in (inside)
next to (beside)
in front of
behind
between
under
around

Unit 3
About Family

Lesson 1
family
father (dad)
mother (mom)
brother
sister
actually

Lesson 2
just a second
phone
notebook computer
headphones
digital camera
online
picture
photo
selfie

Lesson 3
this
that
these
those
umm

Lesson 4
grandfather
grandmother

grandparents
parents
divorced
ex-husband
ex-wife
children
uncle
aunt
cousin

Lesson 5

hang out
hair
color
blond
red
brown
black
length
long
short
facial hair
beard
goatee
mustache
height
short
tall

Unit 4
School Life

Lesson 1

cool
month
January
February
March
April
May
June
July
August
September
October
November
December
date
first
second
third
fourth
fifth
sixth
seventh
eighth
ninth

tenth
eleventh
twelfth
thirteenth
fourteenth
fifteenth
sixteenth
seventeenth
eighteenth
nineteenth
twentieth
thirtieth
twenty-first
twenty-second
thirty-first

Lesson 2

study
read
write
learn
discuss
take notes
practice
take a test
whoa
too
habit

Lesson 3

Monday
Tuesday
Wednesday
Thursday
Friday
Saturday
Sunday
workweek
weekday
weekend

Lesson 4

pre-K/preschool
kindergarten
elementary school
middle school
high school
college
university
1st grade
2nd grade
3rd grade
4th grade
5th grade
6th grade
7th grade
8th grade
9th grade

10th grade
11th grade
12th grade
freshman
sophomore
junior
senior

Lesson 5

wow
in the morning
in the afternoon
in the evening
at night
go out
get ready
have lunch
wake up
go to class
go to bed
go home
have dinner

Unit 5
Doing Things at School

Lesson 1

quarter past three
half past three
quarter to five
seven o'clock
math
English
around
a little before/after
not exactly
a.m.
p.m.
sunrise
wake up
shower
sunset
dinner
club/party

Lesson 2

subject
philosophy
economics
art
biology
history
computer science
French
geometry
physics
music

geography
astronomy

Lesson 3

always
usually
often
sometimes
occasionally
hardly ever
never

Lesson 4

common area
reception
lobby
stairs
hallway
tower
floor

Lesson 5

go
get
take
turn
walk (past)
pass
find
follow
How do I find…?
How do I get to…?
Do you know where…?
How can/may I help you?
Excuse me.
Pardon me.
to/on the left
to/on the right
back
behind
at the top/bottom of
at the end of
until
in front of

Unit 6
Places on Campus

Lesson 1

water fountain
study room
office
computer lab
floor
quiet
clean
big

long
new
fast
empty
dirty
small
loud
slow
crowded
short
old
delicious

Lesson 2

This is…
…speaking.
Can I take a message?
phone number
May I speak to…, please?
Is he in/there?
Sorry, … isn't available.
Talk to you later.

Lesson 3

pool table
bulletin board
vending machine
lounge chair
coffee table
coffee maker
TV
sofa/couch

Lesson 4

front door / front entrance
information desk
bus schedule
student center
How far is it from…?
How much does it cost to…?
It's… from my house to…
It costs… to…
free

Lesson 5

What's up?
Not much.
so (intensifier)
courtyard
dorm
residence
flower
flower bed
bench
grass
tree
shade
sidewalk
walking path

sunny
shining
storm
stormy
windy
cloudy
foggy
hot
warm
rainy
raining
snowy
snowing
cold
cool

Unit 7

Study or Eat?

Lesson 1

heading (going)
right now
nowadays
cafeteria
meal
snack
alone
by himself
together
literature
writer
looking for

Lesson 2

librarian
shelf (shelves)
library card
waiting list
title
subject
author
call number
check out
borrow
return
look for
reserve
due
on loan
due date
check-out date

Lesson 3

pasta
drink/beverage
meat
noodles
stew

fruit
soup
stir-fry
cook
bake
boil
chop

Lesson 4

serve
order
greet
select
seafood
dessert
salad
meat dish
buffet
server
waiter
waitress
menu
item
limit

Lesson 5

coffee
tea
cake
pizza
cup of tea
piece of cake
bowl of soup
bottle of wine
cost
pay
cheap
expensive
in fact

Unit 8

Away from School

Lesson 1

street
address
house
apartment
taxi
car
on foot
bus
subway
walk
take
motorcycle
bike
horse

ride
drive
transportation

Lesson 2

No smoking
Do not enter
Yield
Do not litter
No parking
Stop
parking
trash can
sign

Lesson 3

kitchen
bedroom
upstairs
downstairs
living room
bathroom
home office / study
eat
brush (your) teeth
sleep
cook
do homework
take a shower

Lesson 4

relax
play guitar
watch TV (television)
read a magazine
go to the movies
play video games
listen to music
ride a bike
jog
hang out with friends

Lesson 5

grill
barbecue
burn
dishes
do/wash the dishes
clean
laundry
do/wash the laundry
whine/complain
a while
a short time
a few seconds
a few minutes